# Tell It to My Heart

# Tell It to My Heart

## How I Lost My S#*T, Conquered My Fear, and Found My Voice

# TAYLOR DAYNE

### WITH DAVE SMITHERMAN

**Wyatt-MacKenzie Publishing**
DEADWOOD, OREGON

*Tell It to My Heart*
*How I Lost My S#*T, Conquered My Fear, and Found My Voice*

**Taylor Dayne**
WITH DAVE SMITHERMAN

ISBN: 978-1-948018-30-2, Hardcover
ISBN: 978-1-948018-31-9, Softcover
ISBN: 978-1-948018-32-6, eBook

Library Congress of Control Number: 2018908655

www.TaylorDayne.com

Cover photo by Deborah Anderson
www.deborahanderson.com

All photos are the property of Taylor Dayne unless otherwise noted.

Some names and identifying details have been changed to protect the privacy of individuals. Although the author and publisher have made every effort to ensure that the information in this book was correct at press time, the author and publisher do not assume and hereby disclaim any liability to any party for any loss, damage, or disruption caused by errors or omissions, whether such errors or omissions result from negligence, accident, or any other cause. This book is not intended to provide any medical advice. The reader should consult a physician in matters relating to health and particularly with respect to any symptoms that may require diagnosis or medical attention.

**W**

*Wyatt-MacKenzie Publishing*
DEADWOOD, OREGON

Published by Wyatt-MacKenzie Publishing
info@wyattmackenzie.com

*This is a **Kindle Matchbook** — download the Kindle in color for free
if you purchased the print edition at Amazon.com*

# Dedication

*To my Mother and Father*

# Prologue

My daughter, Astaria, has a beautiful speaking voice. I press the cell phone tightly to my ear the way I used to listen to my transistor radio when I was a little girl. She tells me about her day. Sixteen-year-old girl stuff. Homework. (Real?) Gossip. (Always real.) Who needs to go where, what time, and how she'd like to go see her boyfriend if that's possible. I probe her a bit, specifically about the homework being done. Because until I see it with my own eyes, I don't believe it. Astaria is a remarkably passionate and compassionate girl. Her heart is huge. While her gossip never gets old and never gets mean, her diatribes can go on for what sometimes seem like millennia. She tries to keep a keen eye on everyone around her, and especially her twin brother, Levi. She cares. She notices.

While "book smarts" come at a price for her, what she likes to call her "street smarts" will take her far. I just worry as any mother would about the path she's on, because every day I want to kill her at least once. Her innocence. Her naiveté. But mostly her sense of entitlement. I can't help but SMH all day long thinking *Am I to blame? Is it the cell phone? The computer? Every app she downloads?* As the world gets smaller and smaller and closer and closer, it becomes bigger and vaster and more complicated and quite frankly scarier. So where do you point the finger?

Their generation has everything and nothing at the same time. They think they have all the answers, but not one problem is solved. At least not the problems I believe are important. It makes me scared for them and makes me want to shake them both by the shoulders. It's what hasn't been said that I'm worried about. That's where I'm looking for the next bomb, the landmines I don't want to step on.

For example, coming home the other day from a local west coast performance, I pull up and notice black soot all over the driveway. Upon closer inspection, I can see charred paper and gunpowder residue. The first thought that comes to my mind is: *Levi! I'm going to kill him!*

In less than 24 hours, this kid broke into my bedroom (that's always locked when I leave), got my keys, moved my car, and set off a shitload of bottle rockets in my driveway. (He claims it was only one. I claim bullshit.) Couldn't he think to hose it down so that I wouldn't notice? Of course not.

I call him on his cell while he's on his way to a basketball game in Malibu. "What did you blow up? And don't even think of lying."

This is how I am often greeted. Like a mother bird returning to the nest with food, I never knowing what I'll find when I open the door. I guess it's a form of payback. I remember when my parents used to travel out of town a couple times a year. When we picked them up at the airport, they would say, "We'll go to eat. Tell us the bad stuff first, and then tell us the good."

I'd usually spill everything right away because it would be safer at the diner. It would go something like, "The bad is that the house got robbed, but the good is we got all the stuff back!" or, "I got a summons for disturbing the peace because we threw a party in the backyard, but I know who the judge is because his son was in the band." They would stare at us, usually unable to respond. To be honest, there was never much good news to report.

As Astaria is winding down her story, she reminds me that she broke a string on her guitar. "How much is that?" she asks.

"What, a string?" It suddenly occurs to me that as much as I've worked with guitar players, I've never actually purchased a guitar string. "I don't know, a couple bucks maybe."

She's already moved on to the next topic like a hummingbird whirring from one lilac bush to the next. I listen for a while, not saying much, but in my gut, I get the feeling that something's up.

"Is he there?" I know he's there.

"Who?" She knows who.

"Is Jack there?"

"No."

"Put him on the phone."

"Mom."

"Stop rolling your eyes. I *heard* your eyes roll."

"I'm not putting him on the phone, Mom." Then in a whisper she adds, "That's just so weird."

"How is that weird? I'm your mother. He's in my kitchen, and you are there with him. I'd like to say hello to the person hanging out in the kitchen I paid for."

She says ok, but it's a compromise, putting me on speaker and informing her guest, "My mom wants to say hi."

"Hello?" The guy sounds uncertain but polite. He's the son of a very famous person, and they've been together for a year. It's first love for both of them, and I'm nervous because at 16 I've been there. I know how all-consuming it can be. For my part, I'm just doing the best I can to be a reasonably effective parent. Right now, I'm in "Dad-mode," and the jury is still out on this boyfriend. I guess the jury will always be out. Hell, it's still out on my own kids.

As I'm parenting over the phone, I'm riding in the back of a black Lincoln Navigator over 1400 miles away. I'm about to record a live Instagram feed, and then I need to eat some chicken soup, slide into my black Herve Leger jumpsuit, fix my hair and makeup quickly, and get onstage. What city am I in again? I check the skyline. A spectacular sunset through the smog. Eight hundred degrees in the shade. Traffic backed up for miles. Ah, yeah, Houston. That's right.

My sound check is now two hours and twenty minutes late. I have a small case of anxiety building. I continue making light conversation with Astaria and her boyfriend while I send a text message to my road manager, Will. *What's up? We're very late!! Do these people know what the eff they're doing?* In moments, Will texts me back that he has it under control. I believe him. I know he means it, but there's a little voice in my head telling me we're both in for a surprise or two before this night is over. This kind of festival involves lots of artists and millions of moving parts, and Murphy's Law is always hanging over our heads like a dark cloud.

"How much farther?" I ask the driver, a burly Irish guy with a crewcut. He says it's about five minutes, so I tell Astaria, "Let me talk to your brother. I've got five minutes." I hear dog claws in the background tapping on the tile. I can picture Rufus, my jet-black Pekinese, scrambling after her as she goes to the foot of the stairs to holler for her twin brother.

"Levi! Come to the phone. Talk to Mom."

Levi objects from somewhere upstairs, but I can't make out what he's saying.

"He says he's busy."

"Doing what? Tell him to get on the damn phone."

Astaria hollers, "Levi! Mom says call her. Get on your damn phone." Rufus starts barking his head off. "Mom, Levi says you took his phone."

"Shit. I forgot. Tell him to come downstairs and get on your phone."

"I don't want him touching my phone."

"Astaria, I swear to God—"

"Levi!" she hollers. They stick together for the most part, but she knows I'm not playing around. I hear him trudging down the steps, moaning and groaning.

"Hello."

"Hello. How are you?" I ask very pleasantly. Cordially. Not like someone who now has only three minutes.

"Fine."

"Did you eat? You're invited to Shabbat across the street."

"Really? Can't I just go to Noodle Monster?"

"No, you're invited to Shabbat across the street."

"Mom! Can't I—"

"Shabbat! Across the street! Text me when you get home."

"You took my phone!"

"Oh, yeah. Text me from your sister's phone."

"Why can't you just give me back my own phone?"

"I think you know the problem, Levi. You're not allowed to access those sites. It's an addiction!"

"But having my phone would be for *your* convenience," he says.

"Really? I'm in a fight for your soul, and you're telling me about my convenience? Knock it off and get across the street."

The driver looks over his shoulder and says, "We're here."

"Levi."

"I know."

"No, you don't."

"Yes, I do!"

"Okay, then. We're good, right? Are we good?"

"Yes."

His voice drops a register and it reminds me of a paralyzing truth: I am the mother of a young man. It's scary. I love men. I do. I might not like them very much sometimes, but God knows, I do love them. I used to firmly believe in that knight in shining armor. As a young woman, I was always looking for that iconic male figure. It's taken me years to get to a place where I can love men for who they are instead of who I wish they could be, without me unconditionally handing over the keys to my emotional kingdom. Sometimes my "hope flame" can still make expectations a little too high and my heart a little too open. I have to remind myself of the slow-healing wounds and harsh relationships that I've lived through. It has fine-tuned my BS detector and taught me to rely on myself first, probably to a fault at times. I always shoot for the stars, but that's my nature. I have to strive as an artist to change, to make a statement, to create, to reinvent, to be better, to sound better, make better music, have something more to say.

So that leads me back to Levi. I am trying my best not to project my own bad experiences onto him while raising him to be a good man. At sixteen, he is poised on the edge of forever. He reads a lot and thinks a lot and asks questions on topics like finance, real estate, mortgages, trading. He wonders aloud why the Holocaust happened and how we know if Hitler is really dead and if I've read *Animal Farm*. (I have.) I'm exhausted listening to him. A lot of these questions are just to demonstrate that he knows things, to show he's superior to me. Dear God, he *is* a man. Sometimes I just have to look at him and say, "Really? Do I need to answer that?"

Levi is definitely starting to form his own opinions about the world, and the world doesn't sit still for that. I'm doing my best to help him become a productive member of the most competitive environment I've ever seen. Physically, his testosterone is out there on the football field, but emotionally, he's not there yet. It concerns me because I want him to be the best man he can be, and to me that seems difficult when he is constantly bombarded with unrealistic images of women and graphic messages on his phone, tablet, and laptop. That's what worries me the most because I want my son to know inside what it is to be a good man, what having integrity feels like.

I think a man should be rich in body, mind, and soul. He needs to have emotional and mental soundness. Without that he won't have the ability to form positive, healthy relationships. That's the biggest struggle I have with Levi because for most of his life, I've been the best example of a good man that he's ever had. And I gotta be honest, sometimes that doesn't sit well with me. I'm not comfortable with that yet it keeps me on my toes, always hypervigilant and willing to learn, but it's exhausting. I have to carry the weight. I don't often know the best advice to give him, but I try. I read a lot, research a lot, and talk to my girlfriends, mentors, and counselors.

Anyway, I need to finish up this phone call. I give him the best advice I can think of at the moment.

"Drink some hot water," I tell him. "It will keep your bowels moving."

"You are so weird."

"I know, but I still love you."

"Love you, too."

I can pack a lot of motherhood into three minutes, but it takes a village with these two. Ellie, our nanny, is a sweet, semi-savvy woman who's been with us for a year and a half. She remains on the frontlines while I continue shuttling in and out of town on tours. She's really more of a nurturing chaperone. She does the cooking and cleaning and helps with driving them to after-school activities. She keeps an eye on things and even walks Rufus. It helps a lot because sixteen is tough. Fireworks literally go off when I'm not there—I notice she doesn't even tell me about that. To be honest, my security cameras let me know what's really going on in my home.

My kids are now the age I was when my life seriously went off the rails. Inner demons left me choked and paralyzed as a young woman, a prisoner trapped in my own body and my own head. I look at Astaria and see this beautiful young woman evolving, but I also see a troubled soul at times. I see an anger brewing inside her, even in her silence. It scares me because I was that beautiful young girl once.

As we drive around to the artist entrance of the arena, I can see a line of ticket holders still out front, probably wondering why the show is starting so late. A few savvy hardcore fans are hanging around the backstage door to catch a glimpse of the artists entering through the underbelly of the arena and maybe get an autograph or photo. The car rolls to a stop, and the driver opens my door to escort me backstage. They spot me getting out of the car and head over.

"Taylor! Taylor!"

"Hey there." I wave at them.

One fan makes a beeline for me, and the driver/bodyguard steps between us. Undaunted, the excited fan tries to go around him, holding up a well-preserved 12-inch. It's sheathed in plastic, uber protected—that's a good way to preserve a classic record.

"Could you please sign this?" he asks.

My driver/bodyguard starts to interfere, but I step up and say, "Absolutely. Let's see it."

He hands me the vintage vinyl, my debut album, *Tell It to My Heart,* the original cover. It's like seeing an old friend or a girl I went to high school with. In my heart that girl hasn't changed too much. The album cover is a quintessential '80s moment. There I am: the crimped bangs, the red-painted lips, and strapped into a black neoprene dress with a pie-sliced cutout of skin.

"Wow, how long have you been holding onto this?" I ask him.

"Twenty years. Since high school. You're like the soundtrack of my life."

"I get that a lot." I smile.

He hands me a black Sharpie. I slide the plastic sleeve off the record jacket and write "Love" on one boob and "Taylor" on the other. He looks at the autograph and grins, thanking me. I thank him for coming out and then push through the swinging doors. Now we're on my turf. I know the drill. On the way to my dressing room, I greet the promoters, smile for photographers and venue staff, and chat with local radio DJs and contest winners until my road manager tells me it's time for sound check.

I head to the stage and realize this one's a little different. Oh, man, it's rotating, like a carousel. "In the round," they call it, spinning to give thousands of people a view from every possible angle. Like I said, it's always something. Murphy's Law. I climb the stairs and look out at the seemingly endless rows of seats. As the stage turns, I adjust to the constant motion, hoping it will be less nauseating after I've eaten something. I get a glimpse of Will with the promoter in one of the aisles, not a good sign. I'm guessing Will hasn't collected payment yet.

This is the music business. It's not for the timid, not for the shy, and not for the polite. Sometimes, promoters count on the probability that an artist is not going to walk out of a show and disappoint the fans who've been waiting for hours. It's a mind game. That doesn't happen too often anymore at this stage of my career. It will take a lot more than one skeevy promoter to make me panic. Guys like this remind me of my early club days and early thug days—hustling for gigs, using coat rooms to change clothes, and working in every dive bar from Long Island to Brighton Beach.

I'm just glad I have Will looking out for me while we do sound check. This is a "track show" with multiple artists performing on the same bill, what I refer to as a clusterfuck festival. I sing live to digital recordings, which sound impeccably clear and consistently perfect (usually). It depends on the sound guys in front of house (FOH), and God helps us if there are no monitors. Tracks make for consistent audio. They are cheaper to produce, but honestly, it will never compare to performing live with a band. That's where I shine and that's where I *feel*. When I have a microphone in hand, it's a great night because the one thing I know for sure is that I will be honest with my voice.

I strive for perfection in my sound and tone. We all know nothing is perfect, but I strive for it daily. That's fun for me. The spontaneous moments between me and the fans, that sharing, that movement back and forth with an artist. That's what it's like being live on a stage, moving in a wave of energy between you and your fans.

Will cues up "Tell It to My Heart," I walk over to the monitors and listen back. I sing a line or two, feeling my way into the song like an old friend. I stop the track. "Lose the compression on the mic." I sing a little more and stop again. "Lose a little more." They make the necessary adjustments to the microphone and monitors. "Thank you," I say. "That's better."

I continue tweaking the mix between vocals and tracks. At

this point, some of the other acts are now almost three hours late for the show. The fans are still waiting outside. In my heart, I know it's my job to stay there for them, to perform for them, but they don't know the craziness that's going on backstage. It's a big show involving a dozen groups, and I'm the headliner. I close the show.

I finish sound check, get back into the car, and head to the hotel to eat and get ready for the show. I'm thinking, *this is gonna be a long, long night. I know what they are telling me, but at this rate, I won't go on until one in the morning.* Back in the hotel room, I kick off my boots, slip into a robe, and put my feet up on the sofa. I have a moment to breathe so I dig out the letter I had started writing on the flight from LA to Houston.

*Dear _____,*

*It's been eight weeks since I last saw or spoke with you. Hard to believe.*

I twirl the pen between my fingers like a drumstick. This is harder than I thought it was going to be. Dr. Pat Allen, a renown therapist who specializes in cognitive therapy and empowering women to get out of their own way in romantic relationships, gave me instructions in a private session on what to write in what she calls the "Hi/Bye Letter":

*Paragraph 1: Tell him everything you appreciated and loved about him.*

*Paragraph 2: Tell him what he has done to hurt you.* This is trickier because it's more about what he *hasn't* done. I'm trying to articulate something that isn't there. It's a vacancy. It's a cloud of lost promises that hangs in the air and makes me feel needy. It seems foolish now, in hindsight, that I believed in him. Again.

*Paragraph 3: Tell him what you don't want in a relationship—with him or anyone else.*

*Paragraph 4: Tell him what you do want in a relationship—with him or anyone else.*

*Paragraph 5: And thank him. Thank him for bringing you this painful lesson, which has driven you into therapy, to help you learn how to never, ever, ever make the same mistake again.* This is the part that really speaks to me, because this is now the second time I'm working to get over the same man. This is a rerun of one of the worst episodes in my love life and one of the best episodes in my sex life, but I can't let myself go there right now. I must continue to write.

*You were not present. You live between two worlds, and that's why you feel alone, even when you're lying next to somebody who loves you ... you still feel alone.*

I've given up on this man, but have I given up on love? My heart still pounds inside my chest while I'm writing this. Is that love? Fear? Sorrow? Anxiety? I thought it was essentially a Dear John letter, and I thought I was writing it to the man who'd been turning my heart inside-out in one way or another and making promises and commitments on and off for the last 16 years that he's never kept. Now, as I read and reread the pages—and pages and pages and pages—and rewrite and reread and rewrite, I can see that this is a letter to myself.

A text comes in from Will. *It looks like it'll be midnight.* Ten minutes later. *It looks like twelve-thirty.* I shake my head. Yep, I knew it. It's going to be one o'clock.

*I need a safe place to come home to. I need it like water.*

Thirty minutes later there's a light tapping on the door of my hotel room. "Who is it?"

"Will." It's one a.m.

I let him in, and he pushes an envelope into my hand.

"What the hell is this?" I ask.

"We got paid. Can you put it in your safe?" Will looks unnerved and victorious all at once, like a cat depositing a dead bird at my feet.

"Oh, my God." I roll my eyes. "Sure. Fine." I find the safe in the closet, toss the envelope inside, set the combination, strap on my gladiator shoes and take a final look in the mirror. "Let's go."

In the car on the way back to the venue, I think about Astaria and Levi at home sleeping like angels in their rooms at the top of the stairs while I'm out here singing for our supper. They give me the reason I need to keep going.

As I step onto that merry-go-round stage, I don't worry about my ability to perform for the people who've been waiting for me. My voice is the thing I know I can always count on (thank you God). It has been the only constant in my life of roller coasters and merry-go-rounds.

When I finish here, I'll go back to the hotel for a two-hour power nap, set the alarm for four a.m., and then hop on a plane to meet up with my band for yet another show because that's what I do.

# CHAPTER 1
## *Shelter*

I'M SIX YEARS OLD, and I'm running away. I pack a Shop-Rite paper bag with the most important things I know I'll need—Pop Tarts, pretzels, crayons, construction paper, and my suckie doll. It's late afternoon. I'm scared, but I'm ready to go.

My parents are at my father's office working. I'm not sure what that means, but Mom is there to help with the paperwork. I think that's what happens in an office. My plan is to sneak out while they are gone and go to the Texaco station on the corner to cross that big street, Grand Avenue. I am scared, but less terrified than I am of staying at home.

I'm not allowed to cross any street by myself, let alone the big street. I can feel the sun setting on the back of my navy-blue jumper and green turtleneck. I'm not sure if anyone is missing me yet. I listen hard with my sharpened sense of hearing. Step by step, as I start to walk farther away from the safety of my apartment, the shadows grow longer, and it gets darker.

I huddle with my back against the cool cinder block wall that stretches around the corner to the gas station. Beyond that is the big world. There are no more apartment buildings, no more places to feel safe. I'm not sure what will happen when I cross that street. I'm not even sure where it goes. Will I ever come back? Do I even want to?

IN 1962, I WAS BORN at New York Hospital in the heart of New York City. My parents named me Leslie Joy Wunderman. At two, we moved from the Bronx to the safety of suburban Long Island, with my brother Hugh who was five, and my infant brother, Rob. That was the dream for most young families, especially first-generation immigrants. Being true New Yorkers, we didn't move into a house, but an apartment, more specifically a garden apartment, on Grand Avenue in Baldwin. It was a two-story, three-bedroom unit with a ten-by-ten patch of grass fenced off from the rest of the neighbors, hence "the garden." That was our backyard where my pinto-colored guinea pig named Tarryton could eat in peace.

We lived in apartment #6, which faced the main road. Across the street was where all the action took place. There was a combination muffler shop and gas station, and kitty-corner was the bagel bakery and a luncheonette where I could hear the sounds of a jukebox wafting through the air. My earliest memories are of watching my mother take her mid-morning break. She'd say she was going across the street to the luncheonette for a cup of coffee. When she came home, I could smell the toasted bran muffin with butter that she'd had. With her bell-bottom jeans and wide-rimmed Jackie O glasses, she looked glamorous to me as she left home and went into the sparkling, shiny world.

In my little mind, anything you'd want was right there in my neighborhood. Not only right across the street, but also in the garden apartments, where your neighbors were your best friends by default, whether you liked it or not. Mine were the Wolfs, the Davidsons, the Epsteins, and the Elners—just steps from my front door. To this day, over 50 years later, my parents are still dear friends with some of the families we met at the apartment. I've seen them throughout my life, and they are family. It's unbelievable.

Our apartment complex was full of loud, proud families of many different ethnicities—we had Jewish, Italian, Irish, and African-American. Everybody knew everybody else's business. Us kids were scrappy and most knew how to throw a punch. We would travel around the apartment complex in packs. The younger ones would stick together, older boys would veer off into their own group, and teens were pretending they were already grown up, trying to lose us at every turn.

The summers were beloved. Nothing was ever better than the sounds and smells of our apartment complex pool. Our moms would meet up for Tanqueray and tonics, ice cubes, glasses clinking as everyone lay on lounge chairs smoking Parliaments and Newports like chimneys. Most of them proudly wore colorful bathing caps with dangling decorations that reminded me of fishing lures. The air was fragrant with Coppertone, Bain de Soleil, and baby oil. Some of the sunbathers held silver sun reflectors under their chin as the dads smoked cigars and played poker off to one side.

Over all that noise, I could hear the music of Stevie Wonder, Blood Sweat and Tears, Chicago, and The Carpenters drifting through the air from tinny transistor radios placed strategically around the pool. Then when we heard the familiar warped version of "Turkey in the Straw," all heads popped up. We knew the ice cream truck was coming. There was a mad scramble to ask moms for change. "Give us anything, Mom. Please, please, please." We would charge through the fence barefoot, knocking into each other to get in line, coins held tightly in our sweaty hands. We were always told to bring back the change. How could there be more change from change, I used to think, but there always was.

Even before I learned to swim, I remember carefully navigating off the pool steps and clinging to the cement lip on the side. I was careful not to let go as I watched the older kids play Marco Polo in the deep end. The lifeguard would occasionally blow the whistle at them if the boys got too rough. I loved the water. I loved the smell, that mix of the chlorine and suntan lotion, even after Mr. Shaw, an overweight neighbor with a deformed pinkie finger, tried to drown me by playfully holding my head under the water.

My bedroom window on the second floor of our apartment faced the parking lot. I had the best seat in the house. I could watch the comings and goings of people as they parked their cars, unloaded their groceries, met their wives, called the kids, took out the garbage. As it began to get dark, in the strange twilight, I'd see quick motions around the old tires, under the parked cars. Then they would gather in a swarm to greet each other and investigate the garbage. These stray cats would emerge from behind discarded furniture, under cardboard boxes and through holes in the fence. These herds of feral kittens merged together, yowling and fighting for scraps of food. Some were scrawny and some looked tough. There were tomcats with holes in the fur on their head or around their nose, probably the result of a fight. When the females came around with their little packs of babies, I knew right then and there that I wanted one. They were beautiful. They needed a home. They needed to be loved. I knew they were wild, but I was determined to catch one of those kittens and save it.

For a five-year-old girl, that's a big undertaking, but once I'd made the decision there was no going back. It became my mission to scout the doorways nightly, searching the terrain, watching, creating any excuse to throw out something from our dinner. If someone forgot to put out the garbage, I would offer to take it to the dumpster, so I could catch a glimpse of those wild creatures. It got to the point where I was so desperate, I'd even sneak out after bedtime with my flashlight. I'd watch patiently to catch a glimpse of the skirting kittens with glowing eyes.

I approached this task intensely, the same way I've approached most of the things I really need in my life. God help those kitties! I had to have one and I had to have that kitten love me back. Those were my thoughts, those were my feelings, and that was my certainty. And so it was. Even if these kitties were always just out of reach, too quick or too clever, at some point I was sure I'd narrow the gap. I'd come out scarred, scratched, and dirty, sneaking back inside the house. But my failure to capture one of those wild babies never altered the clarity of my ambition or my future course of action.

This tenacity, this need, this metaphor speaks volumes for a lot of things in my life, like that man for example—the recipient of Dr. Pat's prescription Hi/Bye letter—he looked so beautiful, so fierce, but he behaved wildly and badly when I got too close. Truckloads of self-doubt and unwavering perseverance have led me to every major transformation in my life—the good, the bad, and the ugly. Being raised in a Jewish home, questioning was a big part of our household dialogue. I've searched my whole life for answers to questions that I've constantly raised in myself and others, sometimes maybe annoyingly so, especially if I didn't like the answers. My father always said I was a sore loser. I guess that was true, but more importantly, it led me to always question the answers I'm given.

If you scroll through my queue of favorite shows on any

streaming services, it's obvious that I like ciphers and parables and storytelling. Rarely do I watch nonfiction documentaries. I am a storyteller. A story needs a beginning, a middle, and an end. My life force, the energy in my life, is what keeps me constantly learning and healing. Some call them life lessons. I call it the road less traveled, which I got from the book of the same name by M. Scott Peck. I learned that I've made choices and chosen paths that aren't the norm.

"One who loves must learn fear. One who fears must learn love." I've thought about that quote often. Another one is: "Our mission on earth is to recognize the void—inside and outside of us—and fill it." Like any good Kabbalah student knows, how can we hold all the abundance, all the wealth, all the good, all the health, all the glory, if we don't have a strong vessel? The void we need to fill often does not include the understanding of the cup, the actual vessel we need to build for ourselves. Like my story of the garbage kittens. I wanted to fill that void in myself. In actuality, they never needed anything from me.

I was small and fragile at the time, but I was learning. It's like watching the process many creatures go through. We get to see it with a cocoon, the metamorphosis, the growth, the transformation. They leave something behind, like a snake shedding its skin, which is its vessel. It's incredible, but for humans it's much harder. One of the greatest lessons I've learned is understanding attachment, knowing when I'm attached in a healthy way or a negative one. That's the deep longing to love and be loved. How can my vessel filled with fear have room for love?

One of the things I've learned and understand deeply now is the act of giving, not randomly, but knowingly and with intention. When we are open, our vessels become greater and stronger and able to hold and receive. Ultimately, "the void," the space within the vessel, begins to fill.

Long before I understood this, when I sang, I never felt great. I was so in my head. Over the last ten years, as an established artist, I've learned to honor a different part of myself and not to be on stage for the quick fix of fame. I no longer have to watch a single charting and charting. I realize there's a higher purpose for my voice, and that's the energy it provides to an audience.

Now I'm free to become one with the audience. I am there to

serve. The knowledge of serving, but also being served at the same time, that's the reciprocity. That's the true essence of giving and receiving. Taking all that energy, that attention from the audience, I allow it to fill me now.

Taking all that energy, that attention, and that need is fulfilling and rewarding. When I restrict my ego in terms of what we think of as fame, the rewards come by my understanding of what makes people happy. The answer is simple. My voice. I've watched it transform people. I've watched the ripple effect, the extraordinary turn of energy, the fulfillment, and that has transformed me.

I always get compliments on how I look and how I act young and energetic. It's wonderful, and that comes from my mother. There are plenty of tricks and tools one can use for that, but the most important is the voice within. That's where the breakthroughs are. In my professional life, it became so clear. An audience doesn't reward an artist for holding back. How do you give and fill at the same time? That is the tightrope an artist and entertainer must walk. In my twenties, it often felt like a rope around my neck. If I wasn't charting, if hits weren't coming, I was nothing. If I wasn't selling records, I was nothing. If I wasn't being rewarded, I was nothing. Always trying to outdo yourself, working within the confines of a record company, and being held back creatively goes against the truth of any artist. It soon became my greatest challenge. How can I love myself artistically and professionally?

What started out as a tool for survival became a need to be an artist. I needed to overcome the fears of my past that lived inside of me in order to be here thirty years later and say I'm an artist today. That is the faith that I stand upon. When I'm on stage, I navigate to find the audience's story, to share with them my story, an energy that will resonate higher, so we can all feel better when we leave the show.

Isn't that what teachers and mentors are for? Isn't that why we all search?

I have to believe that there is somethin' I am showing and giving the audience at that moment. I want people to leave feeling better than when they came. On stage as an artist, I took myself out of the mental game and put my heart back into it, and that's made all the difference for me. It has just taken me a while to get there.

MY FEARS AS A YOUNG CHILD were very real to me, my inner peace and preciousness were sadly taken away before I can even clearly remember. My childhood was a blur of hospital stays, physical pain, and emotional terror that developed into a toughness, a separateness, an armor that I still wear.

Our home wasn't often filled with joy and laughter. We were tiptoeing around my father's moods. If he went dark, my brothers and I were hunkered down in whatever corner we could dive into, desperately wanting to be spared from his wrath. It could come at any moment, at any time of the day or night. I would sit alone in my room hiding, cowering. Where was my protection? Who was my knight in shining armor? Where was my hero? Who was my gladiator? It wasn't my dad. He couldn't be. It wasn't my brothers. They had to fend for themselves and hide in their own room. We were all just trying to survive.

Sadly, my mom played the perfect victim, which after a while I wasn't buying. As I got older I refused to accept that as the truth. Even as a child, I could see how a mom must protect. That's her job. I could see that she used my father's demons against him to get what she needed—whatever the hell that was—attention, sympathy. Regardless, she was always curled up in a ball in the corner crying, leaving her children exposed and unprotected. Strength and weakness, fight or flight, it was a vicious cycle, a poisonous snake eating its own tail. Who was in the right? Who was in the wrong? Who was strong? Who was weak? Whose side do you choose when you're tiny and terrified? I ultimately chose my father. He seemed like the strong one to me. That's how I made sense of it as a child and young adult. I pushed my mother away to save my sanity and control my anxiety. I had to believe in something.

I slept with a nightlight and my door ajar until I was thirteen years old, a tool for survival. I had to see whenever someone was coming in order to brace myself. After the nightly fit of rage ran its course, I would often feel my dad's presence in the hallway. It could be 10:00 p.m. or 2:00 a.m. I'd hear him breathing as he quietly entered my room, knelt by my bed, and began to weep. He'd lay his hand on my head and begin to pat my hair. I could feel his tears drip on my head as he whispered, "I'm so sorry, honey. I'm so sorry. You're so special to me. I don't know why I do what I do and say what I say. You're my favorite daughter." He wanted forgiveness. I know that. He wanted peace. I know that. I could *feel* him waiting for my reply.

"I'm your only daughter," I'd say, as if on cue.

He'd laugh softly and say, "You're special. Do you know that?"

Do I know that? Yeah, I know that. His guilt and my fear told me that something set me apart. It gave me hope. I felt that hope flame. Being like other little girls was impossible for me, it only seemed natural that I was different, like many artists say they feel. Being like other girls, like other daughters, like other mothers, like other girlfriends—I stopped trying to connect those dots by the time I was five. I saw it as a positive. I decided I *was* special, and I would continue to focus on that. That kernel of something, that seed of uniqueness, that hope flame that shined like a pilot light was all *mine* and that would be fine. If my mother and father couldn't protect me, I decided then and there my voice would.

My father was a tortured man, and not in a beautiful way. His uncontrollable anger caused him to lash out at the slightest provocation. Explosive, violent, and unable to control his rage, my father tore through our home daily—yelling, screaming, shoving, and hitting.

He was 5'9" with a full head of dark brown hair and piercing blue eyes. My dad always complained about problems with his teeth, and he had a butt like two double-A batteries. Typically, he wore jeans and a flannel button-down shirt with his stomach spilling over the belt and his pants drooping in the back. He and my mother were first-generation post-Holocaust parents, whose extended families had been through great loss, eventually thinning out to only a few remaining fighters and survivors. They both grew up with a brutal understanding of what it was to fight for one's life and to be alone.

My father, by age 26, was a veteran of the Korean War, and had a genuine desire to provide for and protect his family. But he had a challenging upbringing himself. He was the youngest of four siblings with a 15-year age gap between him and the eldest child, with a father in his sixties and a mother he barely knew who was hospitalized often for mental instability.

My grandfather, Harry Wunderman, was into his second marriage after losing his first wife and children in Austria to the plague in the early 1900s. He migrated to the United States as a successful furrier, where he had an arranged marriage in his late thirties to an eighteen-year-old woman, my grandmother.

This family eventually had four children, two daughters and two sons. I've only met one of them, Uncle Bill, who was eight years older than my father. My grandfather was sixty-two when my father was thirteen years old. My father's sisters ultimately raised him after their mother set fire to the house and was sent to a mental hospital, never to return. They were told she had died prematurely, but later he learned that she actually lived in the institution until her death and was buried in an unmarked grave. At eighteen, my father was drafted. When he returned home, he never resumed a relationship with his own family, except for his brother Bill, who had served in WWII.

THERE ARE TWO BATHROOMS in our garden apartment. The one downstairs is a half-bath and at four years old, I can use it by myself. When I am peeing, I notice red in the toilet. I call for my mom. She calls my dad at the office. He comes home and they both look scared. They call the pediatrician who advises them to go to the pharmacy and get a urine sample cup. When Dad returns with the glass cup, I realize that I have to pee again and see that red again. Mom is calming me down while Dad holds the glass cup in his unsteady hand.

I am finally able to go, even though it hurts, and I hear glass shatter. Dad has dropped the cup into the toilet and it breaks. He goes back to the pharmacy for another one. Again, his hands are shaking so badly that he breaks the second cup. On the third trip back from the pharmacy, he is successful, and I am relieved that I can stop trying to pee. We take the sample to my pediatrician who analyzes it and sends us to the hospital to meet a specialist in urology. For the next eighteen years I remain under the care of Dr. Landau.

That began months of increasingly invasive tests, until it was determined that I had some defective plumbing between my bladder and kidneys. My urethra tubes were severely infected, and the toxins were leaking into my body, making my own urine toxic, and leading to kidney infection and potentially death.

There is no delicate way to describe this serious medical problem or the agony, shame, and fear I felt as days and weeks led to a year of tests and probes and fingers and tubes and drugs invading my body. One particularly barbaric test that will forever remain imprinted on my little girl soul was the one where I was catheterized. Try explaining this procedure to a four-year-old who is just beginning to develop a concept of "private parts." X-ray techs, who were almost always men, would take me from my room and help me walk slowly in my flimsy hospital gown down the hallway to the lab. I was cold, and I was naked. I felt exposed to everyone as I hobbled with a tech on each side. Between my legs dangled long rubber tubes and the catheter. I clearly remember each jarring step and the sheer weight of those tubes. I can still hear it like a clanging bell in that fog of pain and humiliation. I felt a great sadness.

They would bring me into a dimly lit room with a large steel table. I was too little to reach it, so they hoisted me up there, sometimes mindfully, more often roughly, because they were in a hurry to shuffle the tubes out of the way and buckle my arms and legs down. They would wheel the IV tree that squawked and rattled like an old screen door as they dragged it over, with a clear bottle of IV solution dangling from a shiny hook. I remember holding back screams as I lay there and watched them attach the catheter to the drip and inject the dye. Then they would leave the room and go into the x-ray booth to avoid the radiation. I always felt it was to avoid looking at me.

The loudspeaker would turn on and I would hear their voices, "How are you doing, Leslie? Are you filling up? Hold on. Can you take a little more?" As I lay completely still, buckled to the steel table, I would stare up for what felt like an eternity, as the solution slowly dripped into the catheter and then my bladder. Sometimes I could answer them and sometimes I couldn't. I wasn't allowed to eat or drink for several hours before the procedure, so my mouth and throat were often as dry as sandpaper. I'd stare at the bottle wishing it could go faster. Small, hot tears dribbled down sideways, a trail that went across my temples and into my ears. I couldn't brush them away because my wrists were bound tightly.

I'd shake my head no, and then yes. "Hold on, Leslie. Try and take some more." Time stood still as I lay there, feeling alone, listening to the *plek plek plek* of the clock on the wall and the *drip drip drip.* Watching that solution became a catatonic state for me as it traveled through the tube and into my bladder. Eventually, my bladder stirred and began to ache.

I stared at that bottle as the ache of awareness became unbearable fullness and then distention which became urgency which became agony. "Just hold it a little longer, Leslie," they'd say over the loudspeaker. Like I really had a choice! I couldn't pee, accidentally or on purpose, when a catheter was pumping solution in the opposite direction. That's not how it works.

"How ya doing, Leslie? Do you feel full yet?"

If I nodded that I was full, they'd say, "Just try to take a little more of the bottle. See if you can hold more. Take the rest of the bottle." After this procedure was done a few times over the course of that year, I learned to just lie there in silence. I learned to endure it though I'll never know how. I'd stare up into those bright fluorescent lights, trying to summon telepathic powers, willing that effing thing to move faster, to stop dripping.

But eventually I couldn't help myself. I always ended up sobbing, begging, pleading with them, telling them I couldn't take any more.

They'd say, "Okay, okay. Hold on." The tech would come in to detach the bottle, and huge X-ray slides would then be swung into place under the table. The catheter would be dragged out of me. "Hold for the X-ray, Leslie. Just a little longer." And on cue, as they ran into their little room to take a photo, like a director they'd say, "Okay, pee."

My little brain would be screaming. I didn't actually make a sound, but I'd clinch my fists and hold my breath. There was no room for so much as a sip of air. I had to do what they said or start the whole thing over again. Then all that agony would give way to humiliation as the solution came out of me, photograph after photograph, x-ray after x-ray, soaking my hospital gown and running off the cold steel table and onto the floor. The X-ray machine whirled and cycled over me, taking image after image.

When it was over, an orderly would come over to undo the Velcro braces, help me down off the table, and redress me in a new hospital gown. Then he would walk me back down the hall, exposed again, where I'd crawl into an awaiting wheelchair, and they would cart me to the elevator and up to the children's ward.

There were other procedures during that year. Not all were hospital stays. Some were more merciful, where I would go under general anesthesia, so I never really knew exactly what was done. Trust me, unconsciousness doesn't mean there is no pain involved. These vivid memories still hold a space in my body and my soul, hence the anxieties I've spent my life working through, a childhood filled with PTSD, leading to panic attacks, and ultimately agoraphobia. When telling this part of my story, I can't help but relive it. It's a sensorial experience. I can smell the Betadine solution, the alcohol, the latex. I can hear the murmur of orderlies and nurses in the hallways and around my bed. With such sadness, my body still retains those memories. Unfortunately, those stretching procedures, as they called them, failed to bring about the results the doctor wanted.

I was five when it is determined that I had to undergo ureteral reimplantation surgery, a major procedure to cut the tubes leading to my kidneys in order to save my life. The surgery involved cutting the infected areas off the tubes and reattaching them. I hope to God that technology is far superior now; I know it is, because this bordered on barbaric. The surgery left a six-inch scar that extended from just below my bellybutton to the top of my pubic area.

My heart aches when I think of the shivering form of a three-foot-tall girl and how courageous I truly was. I can't help but shake my head and feel sorrow for her. After surgery, when I awoke in the recovery room as that fog of anesthesia gradually wore off, I slowly became aware of excruciating pain. I was once again tied down to the bed. Looking around me, my senses coming together, I saw that something terrible had happened to my body.

I realized I was being gurneyed swiftly through the halls, people on either side of me, talking into my ear. When my vision cleared I could see around the room—gowns, masks, green scrubs, two large men cross-talking above me like I was a coffee table. I saw their mouths moving under their masks and felt the rumble of their low voices, but I couldn't make out the words. *Look at me!*

*I'm here! What are you saying? Why am I tied down?* I couldn't see one familiar face with the masks on. I started to really get nervous.

I was then placed in ICU without contact from my family. I was scared and began screaming, "What did you do to me? Look what you did to me!" I thrashed against my restraints and yelled, "Who said you could do this to me? When my daddy sees what you did to me, he's gonna kick your ass!"

There was a moment of suspended belief, as the bustling and chatter stopped, and the room went silent. And then, as if on cue, everyone burst out laughing. People rushed over and started touching me, taking my vitals, pumping morphine into my body. The recovery room busyness resumed, but I was now more than a coffee table. I was a little girl with a mouth who made them laugh. And I can laugh about it now, too. Sometimes a good punchline is the only thing that makes a story bearable. That moment of laughter is a breath of fresh air, oxygen, it gives me a checkmark for another survival tool. Breathing, just like an *oy* or a *vey*, is a breath. I've learned that if you can't laugh, the blackness will take you down. So, I look back, remember that moment, and think, *Ah. Yeah. There was that beautiful little scrapper, the fighter.* I'm so proud of the little girl I was, and yet I'm so sad for her at the same time.

Later, my mother told me that she and my dad were running through the halls frantically trying to get to my room as they wheeled me into recovery. They could hear me screaming down the hall. It makes me think, *Really? What the hell?* I mean, to let a little girl wake up like that? Alone? Of course, I felt abandoned, disconnected, unattached. I was asking for my parents who weren't there. Another parable, I suppose, when every once in a while, you wake up alone and discover that life has torn you right down the fucking middle. But it didn't kill you. Ultimately, it did make me stronger, and that's something. But filling my vessel? No, that I've spent a lifetime learning how to do.

When I was finally able to lift my head, my arms no longer strapped to the gurney, I saw what looked like a car engine where my stomach should be. I saw six plastic tubes sticking out of the gauze bandages. I knew something very bad had happened.

In the ICU, only my parents could visit. Mostly my dad because my mother couldn't drive. After a week, there was a ritual where one tube would be removed at a time. One large tube one day, then one small tube the next over the course of six days. I was not able to be around other patients and the curtain around my bed was always drawn.

After eight days, I was then transferred to the children's ward where there were more nurses and lots of kids. It was a relief. Then I was allowed to have a few things in my room. Most importantly, I had my plastic photo cube with Polaroids of our family—my brothers, my parents, my babysitter. I would stare at the pictures in that cube that represented the summer I was missing out on. There was one snapshot of everyone—my dad, my mom standing there in her mod outfit, Hugh, and just the top of Rob's head because he was little and barely made it into the frame. There was a shot of Jane, the sixteen-year-old who sometimes cared for us. She was draped across a chair looking so much older and wiser and happier than I remembered. My cat Toasty was in her lap with Tarryton eating grass in the background. It was comforting, yet a constant reminder of the summer that was passing me by.

Kids weren't allowed to visit the children's ward back then, so one time my brothers were brought over to stand together outside and I waved at them from my hospital window four stories up. It made me happy to see their faces, but it also reminded me how lonely I was. Of course, I also had my suckie doll. She was balding, only had her left eye, and smelled like old socks. But I needed her. She calmed me. I held on to her tight.

Visiting hours were over at 8:00 p.m. Parents were not allowed to stay in the room overnight in those days. There was no flexibility on that. Rules were rules and the times were the times. My father would come after work, from 4:00 to 8:00 every day. After he'd leave, I'd lie there alone and stare at my photo cube and flip it over and over. I'd look at those photos, waiting for the nurses to make their rounds, eagerly anticipating some Jell-O or ginger ale that came with brief moments of tenderness. Maybe the nice nurses stroked my arm as they took my blood pressure or gave me a shot. Even the stern ones told me I was a brave little girl. I wasn't used to that kind of sweetness and tenderness. It meant a lot. It made my heart open and I felt a little safer.

I'll forever remember those nurses.

It's strange to me that, while I know my mom visited, I recall very little of her presence during my hospital stay. You'd think a tiny child in that situation would be constantly calling for her mommy—clinging to her mommy—I just didn't do that. I loved my mother, and I still do, but I just didn't run to her for shelter or protection. I loved her because I knew I needed to love her, except what was bad about her was very bad. She was not a mother who provided refuge.

My dad, the ticking time bomb, I knew I could count on him to show up. He'd play with me, we would laugh, we would talk about things. Maybe it was because he could drive, and my mom couldn't. He had a car and my mom didn't. All I know is that every day he would come to visit me. He taught me the card game War, and I would always win. Or maybe he let me win. Who cares?

I remember when I was able to finally sit up in bed after all the tubes had been removed, my dad brought me a book called *Curious George Goes to the Hospital* by H.A. and Margaret Rey. When I opened it up, there was a beautiful inscription from my mom. *Dear Leslie, we love you and cherish you. We hope you enjoy this book and it makes you feel better. Love, Mom and Dad.* I still have the book and it is dated 1967.

I was just learning to read then, so I badgered my dad and the nurses to read that book to me over and over again. Curious George was me. Oh, how I loved that book! I loved that little monkey and the Man with the Yellow Hat. He was a saint to me. He was tender and loving to George, even though George was a bad monkey. In that book, George had to get surgery on his belly to remove a puzzle piece that he ate.

I said to my dad, "What a dumbass! Who would eat a piece of puzzle?" My dad laughed. Then I remembered my little brother Rob sticking a puzzle piece up his nose once and getting it stuck, so who was I kidding? Dumbasses all around me, I guess.

In the book, George gets ice cream and lots of attention, and everybody loves him because he "monkeys around" as monkeys do, but the clincher, he made people laugh. And they laughed together. So maybe he wasn't such a dumbass after all!

I started using that tactic myself, and I soon discovered that I could get the nurses to stay in my room a little bit longer if I entertained them by *monkeying around*. I'd crack jokes, tell funnies, little anecdotes, and engage them in precocious conversation. That little ape had nothing on me, because in addition to being funny and playful, I could sing almost any song playing on the radio. That was the summer of 1967, and radio was good. I'm talking AM radio. The Rolling Stones and Stevie Wonder were always playing on the transistor radio my father got me. I could sing along. I memorized all the lyrics. That's when people noticed me and gave me attention for my voice. That helped comfort me as the endless days and nights dragged on.

I spent a significant amount of time in my head, telling myself stories about the glamorous people I heard on the radio. Famous people. They sounded happy, so in my mind, they must be happy. They didn't have to be perfect. Let's face it, Stevie Wonder was blind, but everyone loved him because he could sing. I started thinking to myself, maybe I could be a singer. Maybe I *should* be a singer. Then everyone would love me, too, even though I wasn't perfect. I'm damaged now. So maybe I needed to be famous like a rock star. In my mind, that was the way for me to solve my problems.

So, I became fixated on that vision, some would call it a goal. I fixated on that until it ceased to be a fantasy. It was no longer a pipedream to me; it was really the only future I could see for myself. It became an unshakable certainty that allowed none of the hesitations a child might typically feel about singing in front of people. Alone in my room, on the street, at the store, out on the playground, in the shower, in the car—it didn't matter. My voice would sail out of me without a trace of shyness. I became fearless about one thing in life. My voice.

I was in the children's ward for about a month that summer, which is a damn long time to a little kid. It was long enough for me to change inside, to harden me a little around the edges, and to turn my back on the foolish belief that life could be fair or even merciful. For thirteen years, the catheterization and dilation testing continued monthly, and then it was administered yearly until I was eighteen. Once it ended, the damage had been done, physically and emotionally. My stomach was distorted with raised scar tissue and a smattering of rippled marks left by the tubes and incisions. My ability to carry a child was iffy at best. I'd have to carefully protect my kidneys and everything else for the rest of my life. Truly my Achilles' heel.

Later, after fame, I've had the opportunity to visit children's hospitals for different charities I became involved with over the years. Some of my peers find that very difficult to do. Some of the hospitals are for terminal patients, some not. Neither was an issue for me. I knew how those kids felt. I didn't pity them. I understood that they needed friendship; they needed to feel strong as their bodies fought against them. They needed to feel wanted, to feel a part of the world. As I went to each room and heard the stories from the children or their parents, I'd hold their hands and often we'd sing. Voices are always stronger together. It felt right.

I can still hear the murmur of those voices in the hallways of the hospitals, like white noise. It makes me cry. It's a sadness that runs deep inside me. As a mother, as a woman, as an artist, I've been able to help many children through my gift, through my ability to sing and share that with them. Just like when I comfort those children, I wish I could hold the little girl I was. I want her to feel safe. I want to take away all the pain that I'll never forget.

♭

MY PARENTS HAD NAMED ME Leslie Joy. I'd like to think my middle name was an expression of their best intentions, but after that summer, I was joyful no more. I was still playful, but I had my guard up. A wall had been built.

I started kindergarten in the fall of 1967, and my teacher, Mrs. Davies, was a witch, and not a good witch. A mean, bad witch with white-blue hair piled on her head and a pointy nose. I'd come from such a hellacious, heartbreaking, life-changing medical procedure, and I wasn't sure how much more my vulnerable soul could take. After the first week of school, I begged my mom not to make me go.

"She's just cruel," I told her.

"What does that mean?" she responded. She didn't understand. She was lost in her own world. So every day, off I'd go, walking far behind my older brother to Brookside Elementary School.

Day in and day out, Mrs. Davies would continue to torment the class—yelling, berating us, ordering us to never speak out, to sit down on our mats—and the joy was completely knocked out of me. It reminded me of how I felt around my father on his bad days. What an exhausting way to feel. However, a few weeks into the school year, she did something surprising. In the room there was an old, upright piano that had so far been ignored. She asked all of us to gather around like little chicks at her feet and she began to play. To me, her ugliness disappeared as she asked us to sing a song with her. I don't remember which song it was, but all I know is the half hour of music that took place each day, Singing Time, showed me that there could be some joy at school.

One day during Singing Time, a woman came to the door. She was the choir and music teacher at the school. She was young, beautiful, and stylish, in her late twenties with perfect posture and a refined nose. Her name was Miss Kozowski. To me she looked like an angel, the exact opposite of the devil, old Mrs. Davies. Above her I saw a halo, and I saw salvation.

After listening to us for a while, she left the class without saying a word. Soon after, Mrs. Davies pointed to me. "Leslie Wunderman, please go to the music room." I didn't know what to expect. I walked down the long hallway, knocked on the door, and entered, unsure why I was there. Miss Kozowski was sitting by her piano. She asked if I would be interested in singing with the choir at the Christmas concert. "There's a solo part in 'I Saw Mommy Kissing Santa Claus' that I think you would be perfect for." I couldn't believe it was real. It was exactly what I'd been dreaming school would be like ever since my stay in the hospital. There was only one problem. I was Jewish.

I'd never celebrated Christmas and didn't know much about it except what I'd seen from the other families in our apartment complex. The lights. The trees. The shopping. Endless gifts. And most of all, the Christmas music. However, Miss Kozowski asked me, and I wasn't about to let her down. She was the kindest and sweetest woman I'd ever met, and I wanted to deliver the goods for her with perfect pitch, impeccable timing, and a Jesus-load of seasonal cheer. Whatever she wanted, I would do. I'd even let my classmate Kevin kiss me on the cheek at the finale if that's what she needed for the concert, even though I wasn't sure if I would smile or throw up.

We were a hit. I wore my cute little red apple dress and stood under the bright lights with my patent leather Mary Janes and white stockings, with the sound of the chorus behind me. I became the first kindergartener ever let into the choir.

The next year, I had a new teacher and school didn't seem so bad. Then on my first day of second grade I walked in to see mean Mrs. Davies sitting at the desk once again. I couldn't believe this was happening. I didn't know if I could survive a second year with that woman. By third grade I had another beautiful teacher, Mrs. Esling. She was kind and loved her students like her own since she didn't have children. By the fourth grade, I was put in the glee club, which was filled with sixth-graders, the best voices in elementary school.

Throughout those years, Miss Kozowski continued to be my mentor and worked with me daily as she encouraged my singing and ability to perform. One day, she said I was ready for a solo for the spring concert. She awarded me with a challenging song, a very difficult piece, but she was sure I could handle it. It was "Carousel (La Valse à mille temps)" from the musical *Jacques Brel is Alive and Well and Living in Paris*, which was a big off-Broadway production in New York theater that ran for many years.

The piece was a challenge for a trained mezzosoprano, nothing my nine-year-old mind could wrap itself around, but it didn't matter because I'd do anything for Miss Kozowski. Her passion, her enthusiasm, and her belief in me were everything, and I knew I wouldn't let her down. As we worked together, I practiced my breathing and focused on my control, making the words come out faster and faster with the frenetic pace and melody that continue to build throughout the song.

On the day of the performance as I sat there in my choir robe, I was ready. I took the stage. Miss Kozowski sat down at the piano, nodded at me, and began playing. The piano music whirled, and I soared. The tempo continued to build and build and build, as the carousel spun round and round, finally reaching the frenetic finale. I was excited. Elated. Joyful. I held my breath and looked out at the audience. They were completely silent. Complete silence. Like they were frozen. Then, in a split second, they leapt to their feet, exploding into cheers and applause. It was like thunder.

It was the first time I'd felt that kind of elation, the perfect moment of giving everything to an audience and then receiving in return. It was magical. I had put my entire soul into that performance, gave it my all. I felt the energy of God. And I have been forever addicted to that feeling of elation.

Later, my parents said they clapped so hard their hands hurt. My family, friends, everyone seemed a bit stunned and shocked. They were pleasantly surprised.

"Jack," a friend said to my father, "to hear that voice come out of this small girl!"

"Leslie, you were so amazing!"

"That was unbelievable!"

I tried to take it all in, but it was difficult. I just wanted to go to Friendly's for a holiday sundae. For a long time after, my parents' eyes got wide when they talked about the concert. "You were really something," they'd say in a reverent whisper. I think that was the moment when my parents, that young Jewish couple who left the Bronx and the theatre they loved and cherished so much, started to realize their own child might have some serious talent.

I was so happy that Miss Kozowlski believed in me. I was thankful, and I knew now that this was my destiny. My plan to be a singer was right on track, and here I was, famous at Brookside Elementary School. I'd put in the work. I'd learned the music. I'd practiced every day. At first, I did it for her, but then I was doing for the little girl inside me who felt so loved and cherished through music.

I knew what I wanted to do and now my parents knew. There was no turning back. The wonderful thing was that my parents never stood in the way of my need to be an artist. If anything, they wanted to be part of it. They would ask what they could do or how they could help. That didn't work for my brothers, and the jealousy started to implode in the family because of the focus on me. I never accepted it, though. I had difficulty receiving. My parents wanted to give me the world, but I was afraid to trust their offerings. It was something I had to do on my own. That became my mission statement. That fear robbed me of knowing what support really felt like, what being part of a team can provide. I've had to learn that myself.

This was a private relationship for me. It was my voice, my ear, my talent, my dreams, my ambitions that I couldn't really share with them because they might take it away. I wouldn't share it unless I was on stage in front of an audience. My gift was something private and precious.

My parents never told me that my goal was unrealistic, never urged me to line up something to fall back on. Never drove me away from my passion. They just watched as the train kept going down the tracks. That was their gift to me. It wouldn't have mattered if they had tried to discourage me, but I owe them both a huge thank you for the support they provided through my teens. Some of my friends weren't as accepted at home for their desires and passions—work choices, ethics, sexual orientation. My parents, in spite of their internal demons, were always supportive of us as unique individuals. The arts were revered in our Jewish family and that's what my parents taught me. But I also knew that the rug could be ripped out from underneath me at any moment. I couldn't trust it. In my mind, there was always a catch to the kindness.

From then on, it was often "what does Leslie want?" or "what does Leslie need?" much to the chagrin of my brothers. I never took advantage and they knew that. Still, it didn't sit well with them. I'd say, "I don't want that." I just didn't *take*. As a little girl running away from home, I had decided that I'd never take anything from them. As an adult, that philosophy affected choices in my personal and professional life.

The one constant was our weekends as a family. Saturday was chore day when Robbie, Hughie, and I had to clean our rooms and the bathrooms, and then mop downstairs and run the dishwasher. Sunday was fun day, the one day when my dad was off work, so he called it "family day." I'd pray he woke up on the right side of the bed. I knew we'd have a good day if I heard music coming from the turntable downstairs. There would be soundtracks like *Man of La Mancha* or *The Fantastiks* or Sergio Mendes (*Brazil 66*) playing on the stereo. There was magic coming through the speakers. Then I'd smell breakfast and it would make me smile. This would be a good day.

I'd creep down the stairs, and Dad was usually cooking in the big electric skillet that was used for everything from chicken fricassee to scrambled eggs. On Sunday it was the magic skillet. Red Bermuda onions would be sautéing, sausage and bacon on a nearby plate as the fat dripped on paper towels.

Dad would see me and say, "Everything is done. Are you ready?"

"Really?"

"Let's go, my favorite daughter." It was our special time.

He and I would walk hand in hand down Grand Avenue to the cluster of stores like Harry's Bakery, Arpels Delicatessen, and Woolworth's. This was special. We had the luxury of time as we headed off to Arpels to look at the delicacies like white fish salad, fresh lox, and scallion cream cheese in the glass-enclosed cases. Then he'd stop at the luncheonette to get that huge Sunday *New York Times* newspaper specifically for the *Arts & Leisure* section. It felt like fifty pounds. Our last stop was always Harry's because the onion board bread had to be the last thing we got so it was freshest. I could smell the warm flat bread brushed with egg yolk.

Harry would yell, "Hey, Jack! How you doing? Take a number." It looked like every Jewish family in the neighborhood was queued up for fresh-cut rye bread and bagels.

"Hey, Harry," Dad called back. "I got my special girl here."

"Oh yeah, hi, Leslie. I see her, Jack. Would you like a cookie?"

I'd say, "Yes I would."

That's when I'd get a bowtie cookie. It was flaky like a cannoli, and I'd suck the crusty sugar off it, letting each crystal melt in my mouth. Dad and Harry would talk for a bit, and then Dad and I would start home, juggling bags of food and the treasures that we had collected. I held my prized cookie tightly. Those were the good Sundays. If Dad woke up on the other side, that would be a dark day, but most Sundays he didn't and that was a good thing.

With my kids, I still celebrate Sunday as family day. No matter where I've been, I usually fly early Sunday to get home because it's our day together. They are teenagers and God knows they'd rather be anywhere else in the world, but that's family day. We go to brunch, I cook, we go to dinner, we have friends over. Even when they complain, I know it's something that will help glue them to our family and friends. Our traditions will mean something to them as they get older like the way we sit on the edge of my bed and decide what we will do for the day. I cherish it more than anything.

After my dad and I would return home on those Sundays, the family would jump into our tank of a car, a Mercedes-Benz with rounded edges that reminded me of a submarine. It was a complete lemon and broke down every other day. Still, we'd load up and head into New York City every Sunday without fail. My parents were avid theatergoers and remained members of off-Broadway theatres like the Manhattan Theatre Club, The Roundabout Theatre, and Joseph Papp. That was the greatest joy in their lives.

I loved going into the city and eating in Manhattan or the Upper East Side. We'd go to Chinatown or Little Italy and learn something new each time. When the Wunderman family went into a restaurant, my father would glow. He'd walk in like a king and we'd follow like little ducklings. Most Sundays were good, but anything could trigger my father's displeasure—a wrong move, a wrong word.

My father loved when the maître d' would usher us to a table. It made him feel so important. I saw how much that meant to him. He loved the recognition. He liked to be seen. Depending on the restaurant, sometimes the chef would cook fish especially for him, just the way he liked it. My dad would suck on the head and tail like he was still in Korea.

It was a ritual that my dad would order a hot and spicy sea bass, the whole fish for himself. Then we would watch in complete disgust as he would rip off the head, sucking on both ends and putting the waste in another bowl with one hand. With the other, his chopsticks would never stop moving as the ever-present bowl of rice rested just below his mouth to scoop in the fish.

Finally, I got up the nerve to ask, "Dad, can I try a piece of the sea bass?" He looked at me over the fish with a low growl, but finally gave in. He told me from that day on his Sundays were ruined, but always said it with a smile and a chuckle. He said I had destroyed any bit of peace he had with his sea bass. I promised he could still suck on the head and tail, but I was going to eat that sea bass with him from then on.

When we went out for dinner during the week, things didn't often turn out so well. We'd go to Sizzler and Hughie would get that warning from my mom not to order an extra Coke. As Dad returned from the buffet with a full plate, his voice would always get loud enough to rattle the pots and pans in the kitchen. He would scream at us no matter where he was. "What'd I tell you last time, huh? What did I say?"

Everyone would look at us. Every head in the place swiveled in our direction. My embarrassment would make me sink me further into my seat as I felt the stares and heard the whispers. *What a mean man!* Dad never cared about the audience around us. It didn't matter to him. He was the star. I kept thinking, *it's coming, it's coming. Just let me get through this meal. Hopefully he won't do any hitting when we get home.* My mother rarely said anything other than acting shocked and letting out small sounds of *oh* or *ooh* as my father lashed out. She'd make feeble attempts to calm him down, which was like trying to tunnel out of a prison with a spoon. It never worked. The only thing worse than sitting there was knowing that by the time we got home, my father would usually go into in a full-blown rage. Screaming. Slapping. Throwing things against the wall. Doors slamming. In and out of the house he would go, jumping in his car, driving off, and coming back home. I would look out my window to check the parking lot to see when he was coming back, trying to protect my soul. It was chaos. It was war. I was in a battlefield. I developed severe PTSD as a result.

I never got the sense that Mom saw herself as part of the show. While the drama often erupted in our home several times a week, I felt like she was always playing an audience member. She knew the victim role very well, never saying *stop* or *get out*. Eventually she'd crumble against a wall in the corner and cry.

My mom's mother, Helen Harris, hated my father's guts. She was a small Polish woman who spoke very little English—and even less as she became increasingly senile—but that didn't stop her from screaming in Dad's face as my mom lay on the floor. Only 4' 10", she'd yell in Yiddish and English for him to get out. Having escaped from a world where Nazis were killing families by the thousands and where she lost her own relatives, she wasn't afraid of anything, and definitely not my father.

When my father got physical, Hugh was usually on the receiving end. It's never acceptable to bellow in your child's face that he's a useless piece of shit. It's inexcusable, it's sad, and that's how we suffered. My father never offered any excuses. I don't think he understood what he was doing to us. Years later, he's had enough therapy to know how damaging that had been. He discovered that he was robbed of his own childhood, and that left him angry, barren, vulnerable, and scared, which manifested in his fits of rage. I pitied him more than I did my mother. I saw her fall apart while my father seemed the stronger one. I will never understand a mother not protecting her own. I grew to silently hate her for that. My father seemed stronger even though he was the perpetrator. I gravitated to where I saw strength instead of weakness.

Mom was definitely abused emotionally and sometimes physically, but I felt she was also complicit in this dysfunctional mosh pit by failing to protect her children and instead serving her own needs. That's how it felt to the little girl cowering on her bed in the corner of the room, crying, trembling, holding her stomach in knots, waiting for the door to slam for the last time. The overly sensitized eventually becomes desensitized. At least that's what it was to me. I was constantly in a fight or flight state, all because of the rage and fear and sorrow I held inside of me.

Today, I still have a hard time getting past those feelings. Some days I'm more successful than others. As a parent myself now, I've learned to look at my mother with more compassion. I hug her, I love her, she is my mom. Still, I have a hard time getting past the past. It's hard for me to take her in. There's so much of her. I feel forever robbed of getting a mother's love the way I *needed it* as a child. Yet today my greatest fear is to hear that she or my father has passed away. I finally have a feeling of attachment to them. The relationship we have now gives me incredible comfort. Every day that I can speak to them is a blessing. I even save all their voice messages on my phone.

I often wonder when my mom started owning her own power. When did she make that decision? Was it when she went off to learn about herself? Maybe that discovery came with a sense of ownership in the damage that took place in our childhood. Or did she go deeper into her own childhood, feeling more a victim of her own circumstances? That's where her weaknesses lie. She still likes to say *I'm a bad girl* in a baby voice when I am mad at her. I can't get the image out of my head. How the hell did this woman raise children? Everyone around her says she's the most loving person, never says a bad thing about anyone, but I saw the other side. I saw her crying, self-absorbed, addicted to my dad's behavior.

As a mother, I can understand that now better than I ever did growing up with her. I recognize there is a voice in each of us, a song, a cry, a scream. We learn to either ignore it or honor it. My mother let hers out. She sang. She's not the shy one, but her voice was as needy as mine was free. As I carved that freedom for myself, my voice was the tool that helped me do that. My God-given gift, the key, that seed, gave me my specialness. Still, it took a lot for a little girl to decide to only trust herself. I made courageous choices as a child watching my mother cowering in the corner while somebody beat her kids. I decided that woman would never be me.

Every day as my brother Hugh begrudgingly walked us to school, as we passed house after house after house, I'd play the "I wish" game.

> *I wish I lived in the house with the blue shutters.*
> *I'm sure everyone is happy there.*
> *I wish I lived in that big white house.*
> *I bet they have kittens, and lots of 'em.*
> *I wouldn't want to run away from there.*

## CHAPTER 2
# Don't Push Me

STARTING JUNIOR HIGH was like starting over. New bus stop. New friends. New school. New house. We had moved over the summer. No longer were we in the garden apartment. We had our own house and my parents had finally "made it." My mom and dad promised that I'd make friends in our new neighborhood. They were concerned with social justice, so we moved to a neighborhood that was in the midst of regentrification. They made sure that we were in a very integrated area. We were right on the border of two schools, Baldwin and Roosevelt. I found myself once again between worlds.

At the bus stop the first day of school, I met a couple of girls also entering their first year of junior high, Polly and Erin. Who knew waiting at a bus stop could lead to a lifetime of friendship? So much anticipation, desire, and interest. Erin was a brilliant wordsmith and Polly had the bluest eyes and most beautiful smile. We soon called ourselves ELP for Erin, Leslie, and Polly, but also as a tribute to a band we all liked, Emerson, Lake, and Palmer.

Everything revolved around the integration of fashion and music. We loved looking at magazines like *Rolling Stone* and were mesmerized by the models that were often dating the singers, like Jerry Hall and Patty Hansen. It was clear that beauty, fashion, and rock n' roll music went together. Music dominated our world and we would discuss the lyrics intently as Erin wrote them down and Polly drew intricate images.

Every day at school, we were on display and we focused on our looks—worn-out Levi's with random macramé patches sewn on, floppy hats with a leather brim, and feather earrings that we'd find at head shops. They always had the most unique jewelry and we loved the smell of incense and the great music that was always playing. It was an incredible time with lots of new experiences. It was really what we read, what we heard, what we smelled, and what we saw. Our senses were so keen.

I made sure to stand out in a way that made me feel powerful. I had a monthly ritual where I'd create a mixture of ingredients that I got from the health food store, cover my hair in plastic wrap, and sit in the backyard under the scorching sun, making sure I got just the right amount of golden hues. The next day I'd strut through school rocking my shimmering, highlighted hair as it cascaded down to my waist. The hot, older girls would corner me in the bathroom. "What did you do? Your hair looks so good." I knew that was magic. I'd made an impression. That was powerful. Popularity was a scoreboard and I wanted to rank high on it.

I always had an eclectic group of friends during this time. I learned that safety comes in numbers. After watching my brother get his ass kicked every day in school, I knew that the cool crowd was where I wanted to be. I would never allow myself to be alone and to be bullied like that. I would hang out with the jocks, the dirt bags, the popular kids, even the Dead Heads who impressed me with their street smarts and that made me feel protected in some way.

Music allowed me to have these liaisons with different school groups because of my voice. I was also a good athlete with a competitive nature. I put in the work to focus on my voice and participate in gymnastics. (I was told at a young age that I didn't have a body for ballet.) I learned early on that looking good was important (even when I didn't feel pretty). It was necessary to make a good impression walking up and down the hallways between classes, hoping to get noticed by the hot guys. When someone made a comment like "look at her," it was a form of power and I enjoyed that. I needed it.

The one thing I did consistently was devote myself to my voice. I listened to all musical genres that sparked energy inside me including Neil Young, The Allman Brothers, and bluesy swamp music. I would feel the lyrics of someone like Joni Mitchell. I'd never heard visual landscapes like the ones she sang about.

I believed her words and began to live through them. On her album *Blue* I keenly listened to every nuance in her voice. She had perfect pitch and I was mesmerized by *Ladies of the Canyon*. I wished I had a river I could sail away on. I even chose to perform "River" as a solo in my tenth-grade performance for Dr. Melinda Edwards, my choir conductor.

Being in the choir wasn't considered cool, but I was an exception to the rule. Singing Joni only added to my cool factor. However, I didn't understand how impactful she was to an entire generation. I was just drawn to her music. I was crafting my voice into an instrument and making it a tool that would lead me to the next chapter of my life. It helped that I had a great mentor in Dr. Edwards. Her power and dedication were an important part of my work ethic. I saw the passion in her smile every day during the required music class. I was among a group of one hundred choir students including football and lacrosse players. We all sang as one. Dr. Edwards understood my talent and as a mezzosoprano she asked if I would sit in with the tenor section. I took that as a compliment. When I noticed that I was between the jocks, I was even happier.

Our energies merged, and we soared in unison, culminating at the annual Christmas concert where she would invite her choir alumni to come on stage to sing the *Hallelujah* chorus at the end of the show. There were students who had graduated 10 or 15 years earlier running to join the stage and sing for her. It became even more exciting as some of her previous students became more recognized, including Dee Snider of the group Twisted Sister. I thought, *one day I will come back as a recognized alumnus and celebrated vocalist.*

All my life I've been told, *I love your voice,* or *You have such a beautiful voice,* or *That was an amazing performance.* I know they were showing their appreciation, but it was always difficult for me to receive and process compliments. I spent many years working to develop my inner voice to be able to process the feedback that my singing voice generated, especially as the audiences grew from family members to large auditoriums of people I didn't know. For some reason, I always felt like there was an agenda attached. I spent years working on developing my inner voice to be able to process the feedback, both positive and critical. I needed to think differently so I could be more coachable. I wanted to learn and develop so that I could improve and find my purpose.

Growing up, I was always told "don't take" or "you can't ask" or "you can't get." The attention I received as a child ranged from hospital stays to rants from my father. So later, when I was given encouragement for my voice, it felt like a warm hug; but I was always waiting for the slap. It was like when my father came into my room with tears and sensitivity and tenderness after I had endured the chaos. He wanted to be absolved, but that cycle just hardened me. I became a statue inside. Even when I achieved fame, I wasn't able to properly receive that love from fans or fully appreciate the financial rewards. I couldn't take it in without feeling undeserving on some level. I finally learned that the less I am attached to outcomes, the easier it is to receive. Lessons like that came by doing the work, immersing myself in the sacred Jewish holidays and traditions, studying techniques like kabbalah to discover my purpose, and investing in my mental health.

Reading became an important part of my daily activity. I could lose myself in the story and become someone else. I was a voracious reader; I sometimes had three books going at once. It was an escape. My ear for storytelling evolved alongside my ear for music. I'll never forget when I started reading *Watership Down* by Richard Adams. It was an advanced book for my age, but the deep messages and hidden metaphors were so clear to me. There were societal breakdowns and class systems—much like how I felt in the junior high. What an incredible experience it was to read the description of an underworld of rabbits living like humans.

I'd go through the bookshelves in my parents' room and borrow paperbacks. They had all the latest and most controversial titles like *Fear of Flying* by Erica Jong. One that really caught my attention was *Even Cowgirls Get the Blues* by Tom Robbins. It was a difficult book for me to wrap my head around. It was about a girl with oversized thumbs that are considered a handicap, but she sees them as a gift. Reading gave me an insight and ability to see things on a larger scale, to speak a language with more depth, to see the world differently. Reading to me became as powerful as listening.

By the 10th grade, I was throwing up daily. I'd eat my one meal of only vegetables and soy sauce. It was all trial and error, sometimes bingeing, maybe eating six peanut butter and jelly sandwiches. I learned how much time to wait between certain food types before I could purge. It was another tool to help me gain control over my environment. When you force yourself to throw up, you're pushing out at the same time. It is incredibly draining. I knew I had a higher purpose with my voice and how damaging this was, but it was compulsive. My weight, my looks, my need to be in control took precedence, but I knew this had an expiration date. If I truly wanted to sing, I couldn't continue this self-hatred. I'd have to get control over my food, my diet, and myself. Erin took it a step further. She was crash dieting and working out until we didn't even know who she was anymore. She went down to 88 pounds as we were all navigating a confusing time of insecurity, dating, being included, being left out, feeling pretty, feeling ugly. We were a sisterhood. We shared our fears or anxieties. We made promises to support one another. Our bonds were real and undying.

Among the three of us, Erin started smoking weed first. Once when she and I smoked at her house, I got a strange feeling of anxiety and even started hallucinating. I looked at her and she seemed to be outside of her body. Then it was like I was outside of myself and I could see the bones in my neck opening and closing as I took each breath. I could see every molecule of moisture coming out of my open trachea and it scared the living shit out of me. I thought I was really dying.

I said, "Erin, I'm fucking dying! Let's go tell your mother."

She said, "No! Sit down! You know, we can't tell my mother. Hold on. I have something for you."

I started running around the house like a chicken with my head cut off. "We have to get to the hospital!"

Erin said, "Wait, look at this."

I could feel the beads of sweat, the nausea. I felt like I was trapped in a nightmare. "What are you doing? What do you want to show me?"

"Look at this, it will help distract you."

She handed me an acorn. "Are you shitting me? An acorn?" I threw it at her, hitting her on the cheek, and ran out the door and down the stairs. I could hear her yelling, "Don't tell! Don't tell!" I bolted out the front door and it was like I was out in the wild.

When I turned around, Erin blasted me with the garden hose, knocking me to the ground.

"Help me throw up. Help me throw up. I think I will feel better!" Finally, my panic attack subsided and Erin was right there with me.

She said, "The next time you have an attack, I'll know what to do."

"The next time? There ain't going to be a next time!" I knew then and there I couldn't handle weed anymore. That batch was probably laced with Angel Dust. Back then, anything was game. It was clear that pot was no longer my friend. That's when they started calling me "one-toke Les." I could take one little hit or just sit in a car with them and get stoned as an MF on a contact high.

Fortunately, in New York at that time, the legal drinking age was 18 so that was my way to escape. By high school, fake IDs were as common as toast in the morning. We all used them to get into the clubs because that's where we could hear live music. On weekends, it was not unusual for me to be in a bar with my patch pants and feathered earrings at age sixteen. We were able to see local bands play music, and that's what we loved to do. I'd knock back a Tom Collins and soak in the atmosphere.

When I started dating Noah, I was almost sixteen. He was my first serious boyfriend, my first true love, my first everything. His father was a set designer who owned a huge warehouse full of props in Queens called Silvercup Studios. His mother was a poet and writer. They had an amazing house on the harbor where both parents lived even though they were divorced.

We met in the school quad when he introduced himself to me and said, "Hey, I heard you sing. I'm starting a band."

The attention made me feel good, especially coming from an older boy. I mean, he could even drive! He flashed a beautiful smile and said, "I'm starting a band and I'd love for you to try out. I can come pick you up."

I was a little nervous but excited. As promised, he picked me up in a VW camper bus. I could hear the gears grinding three streets away. He pulled up in front of my house and slid the door open for me. I felt like a queen climbing into the front passenger seat. This was the big time! We drove to a beautiful Spanish-style house near the harbor. There was a cathedral ceiling in the entryway and the furniture was incredibly ornate. The living room was completely filled with music equipment and even had a small stage. It was like Wonderland.

"This is your house?"

"Yeah," he said. "We rehearse right here." It was magical.

As Noah continued to take his guitar playing seriously, I knew this was where I wanted to be. He turned me on to music and artists and musicians who wouldn't have necessarily been in my wheelhouse. He gravitated toward musicianship and bands that were more fusion and rock-oriented like Jeff Beck and Stanley Clark and Chick Corea. At first, I mainly listened to support him, but then I started to really appreciate the talent. As he showed me what inspired him, I couldn't help but naturally lean in. When he started playing Jimi Hendrix for me and asked if I could learn the solos, I was mesmerized. The music was deeper, darker, with cord structures I'd never heard before. I listened with such intensity, and I would sing the solos back to him note for note, so he could pick them out on his guitar. It was this wonderful, intimate, creative time that we shared together. We created our own world and it was beautiful.

He took me to my first concert, and I became more immersed in the music. I was obsessed with the biographies of artists like Hendrix and Neil Young and Stephen Stills. I'd read their stories to learn how they found fame and stardom, how Joni was discovered in a coffee shop. I was also listening to the radio and buying records of my own. I'd lie down in the middle of the living room in front of my parents' huge console stereo system and quietly listen to one side of Pink Floyd's *Wish You Were Here*, paying attention to David Gilmour, note after note. It gave me feelings I'd never experienced.

Long Island had a rapidly-evolving music scene. As I became more aware of what was going on musically, Noah and I would drive to the clubs that had once seemed so far away. One place that we passed by often as we drove up and down Grand Avenue in Baldwin looked like a storefront except there were always cool, funky-looking guys standing outside smoking cigarettes and wearing tight jeans and leather jackets. I found out it was a rehearsal studio owned by the DiBenedetto family. A couple of the kids went to my high school. Several local bands that recorded there were starting to make some noise. Twisted Sister. Joan Jett and the Blackhearts. The Stray Cats. They were all breaking within a twelve-mile radius of where I grew up, and that was very exciting. It gave me the feeling that anything was possible. That magical studio was where I wanted to be.

That summer, my parents decided to send me on a European bike trip. That's when darkness and depression overtook me like I'd never experienced before. My fears became so real because I was consumed by daily anxiety just thinking about going to Europe. Originally, Erin was going with me, but she bailed out. I realized I'd have to go on this journey by myself. Fear was living large within me.

When I went on that trip, my life seriously changed. Later, I described it as a Tour de France meets *Lord of the Flies*. My parents thought they were opening me up to a world of beauty and culture and diversity. In reality, I traveled with a pack of privileged NYC private-school kids who I'd met at a travel agency called the Youth Hostel. We were going to experience France on a bike, one hostel at a time, through the Loire Valley. All I saw was several weeks on the calendar that would take me away from my boyfriend and the people closest to me. Once again, my summer was gone. Leading up to the trip was a daily navigation of anxiety and panic.

I would say to Mom, "I don't want to go. Erin dropped out. Why do I have to go?" I should have fought for what I wanted, but I felt almost as helpless, hopeless, and victim-filled as I had been in that hospital going through those surgeries. *Just stay strong. You'll get through it.* I didn't want to say I was too scared, and that I didn't want to go that far from home. I didn't want to leave Noah. However, in our house, if you couldn't deal with something, that meant you were weak. And that was too much like my mom. So, I took my duffle bag, knapsack, and bike to New York to meet the group.

Our "counselor" was a 25-year-old woman leading a group of five girls and six guys, all of us planning to bike through the wine vineyards in the Loire Valley of France. It sounded so magical with the description of chateaus and villages. It was intended to expand my views of the world, to see beyond the Long Island Expressway before I went off to college. A part of me truly wanted the adventure and the freedom, because that is part of being a rock star, but my true soul was scared to death.

The trip started out with promise as we met up at JFK and flew together. Among the pretty girls and cute boys, one guy stood out as a Leonardo DiCaprio type. He was handsome and playful, yet seemed serious, older beyond his years. His brother and sister-in-law were his guardians since his parents had passed. And another boy stood out, one who had special needs, and I knew he wouldn't last long.

I felt out of place right away as a Long Island suburbanite among these kids from Manhattan. After the first few days, things started going downhill. We all almost immediately began to drink like fish, even the counselor. We went from staying in youth hostels to sleeping in tents that we set up in farm fields along the way. Soon, the counselor was involved with one of the boys. It just felt like we had been dropped on an island and left to our own devices. We were quickly going off the rails.

In order to feel safe, I attached myself to the boys. I felt very alone because my fear felt so real. I couldn't talk to anybody because it wasn't like we could call home whenever we wanted. We had four designated stops along the trip where we could pick up mail and make a collect call (from France!) if we wanted to. I got one letter from Noah during the first week. I held that letter close to my heart while I sang sorrowful Joni Mitchell songs in my head as we biked mile after mile on dirt roads along shit-filled pastures where we would sleep at night. I had attached myself to the Leonardo kid who then said that he wanted to go home. I looked at him. "You're the strongest person here and you're bailing?" The special-needs kid was already gone since he had trouble keeping up with the group.

The night before Leonardo was planning to leave, the two of us ended up alone by our tent in a pasture drinking beer. Soon we were fooling around a little, nothing serious. After we'd been intimate, and I finally felt connected to someone on this insane cross-country trek, he was getting ready to leave. It was strange to me that he didn't seem to have a problem with that. He didn't see quitting as a weakness like I did, and he seemed the strongest of all.

The next morning, with sunshine in our faces, I felt that familiar wave of nausea. Perspiration started beading on my face and trickling down my skin. Before I realized what was happening, I was hyperventilating. I had to get up. It was all too much to bear. Why was I even here? Do I need to go to a hospital? The craziness of the trip, the counselor, the uselessness of it all, Noah not writing more, my feeling of isolation—I had what I found out later was a full-blown, honest-to-goodness, certifiable panic attack in the middle of that cow-patty field on an isolated farm in the middle of the Loire Valley.

I later learned the term astro-projection. I felt myself floating above my body. It was like my body no longer worked. I didn't want to show fear and panic, so I asked the boy to hold me. It was the only thing I thought could anchor me. I knew I wouldn't be able to control myself. This was the first time it had happened in daylight, without any pot involved. I thought I was going crazy. I could no longer associate the attacks with pot. It was now part of me. I thought I was losing my mind. He was holding me and trying to calm me down, but I had no clue what was happening. I felt so scared, and I was embarrassed that I had to ask for help. I never liked to ask anyone for anything.

Finally, I was able to regain control of myself. I realized at that moment that since I wasn't going to bail on the trip, I'd have to handle this problem. I pulled myself up by my bootstraps, rolled up my sleeves, and became my own drill sergeant. I told the girls we were checking into a hostel that day. "We're all going to shower, we're going to pack, do our wash, and then go to sleep—and not drink." Just like after my surgical procedures, I was laser-focused on taking care of myself. I was determined to see this trip through to the end, despite my thoughts of possibly ending up in a mental institution. At the end of that day, Leonardo got on a bus back to Paris. Then there were nine.

On the last day of the trip, while we were waiting along the walls of a Belgian train station, our bikes and other possessions were stolen. I only had my fanny pack and passport. I felt small and broken. When it was time to leave, we were a sad, disheveled caravan muddling through the airport with our few belongings. We traveled back to NYC bonded through our scars. Even our flight was delayed. I never spoke to any of those kids again.

I was picked up at the airport by my parents, but I didn't have much to say. After we arrived home, I asked my mom privately if she would come with me as I drove to Noah's house. She said, "Okay, honey." It was around 4:00 a.m., my internal clock was off anyway. When we arrived, I walked to the back of the house and noticed the light in his room was on, which I thought was strange. I had planned to wake him and say "Hi, I'm home." It felt like I had been gone forever.

I tapped on the window, and when he opened it, he looked like he'd seen a ghost.

"I'm back," I said.

"Hi," he said solemnly. "Let me open the door. I'm getting ready for work." Since he'd just graduated, I wasn't aware he had started working full-time. That wasn't in the letter.

As I walked to the front door, I felt change within him. We went to his room and I asked, "How are you?" but he wouldn't even look at me.

"Leslie, I'm sorry, but I broke up with you. We're not together anymore. I'm dating someone else now."

"What?" I couldn't believe it. My heart was beating so fast. I felt the nausea coming on.

He said, "Sorry, but I broke up with you."

"Is that why I haven't heard from you? When did this start?"

"I don't know. A few weeks ago."

"A few weeks ago? Who?"

Then he told me. It was the sister of a friend of ours. She was twenty-two years old. That was a woman. "You're dating her?" I got up, collected my heart, and walked out of the house. The same feelings of being extracted from my home were the same feelings I had then. I wanted to run away. The last few weeks had felt so surreal that now it seemed like the one thing I thought I could count on was gone. I felt completely empty.

"Mom, can you drive us home?" I had nothing left.

I went to my room, got in bed, and I slept for twenty-four hours straight. I was depleted emotionally, physically, and mentally. Spiritually, I believed in nothing anymore. I had a new reality. Everything that was, now wasn't. Romantic relationships were now added to the long list of things I would never trust again. Noah was the one who had been so sure about us, so it was devastating that he broke up with me.

When I came home from France, I was certain love would be waiting for me. After everything I'd been through in Europe, my heart just couldn't take it. I was shattered. First, it was at home where the hand that hugs is the hand that hits. Then in the hospital what's supposed to heal you is the thing that's hurting you the most. I'd already had to suspend belief and learn who to trust and how to trust. That plagued me through most of my life.

Going into my senior year, I slowly recovered from that summer in Europe. I reconnected with my girlfriends and the wounds that were gaping and open and raw were healing to some degree, but not my soul, not my emotional landscape, not my anxiety that was still deep within me. I became much more disciplined about eating and exercise and sleep, knowing that I could lose control at any time. My social circle needed to expand because ELP would be breaking up soon, with Erin taking early graduation and going to Cornell. The things I had always known were now changing. One thing was clear to me: I was never going away or doing anything else against my own will again.

I decided I was not going away to college. I would go locally. My parents were devastated, but I knew that I couldn't possibly handle it emotionally. Nassau Community College had a good music program, and I would study voice and opera and classical music. Some of my high school friends would also be attending, so I felt like I could cope with that.

I was determined not to let anyone push me into something I didn't want to do anymore. I would have to control my choices and my surroundings, the way I felt when my father would have one of his episodes. That's what put the mental prison bars around me that I could not escape. The greater loss was that I knew I was no longer free. Not being able to travel meant that I couldn't follow in the footsteps of the artists and models on *Rolling Stone* covers that stared back at me from my bedroom walls. I admired them because they seemed so free. This was becoming a prison that I didn't want to escape. It was the only place that felt safe to me. Yet I knew that just like those famous people on my walls, at some point I needed to.

When I was a senior, Hugh was a sophomore in college and Rob was in the 11th grade. Tension, hostility, and anger was resonating at a higher frequency in my home while my mother was

TAYLOR DAYNE
38

going in and out of the city to attend her theater and music classes and my father was retreating to the security of his office. When Hugh came home for a school break, we decided to throw them a surprise 25th wedding anniversary party. Two weeks after that, my father told us he was leaving and filing for divorce. I was thinking *couldn't he have done this ten years ago?* It was a rude awakening. By throwing the party, we were honoring something that they hadn't really honored themselves. Suddenly, we were caught in a film noir. My parents had trapped us in that house for all those years. Now we were all in suspended animation, everyone stuck in time, like the frame hadn't flipped, exaggerated moments of fear and anger and hurt. My father left, and even though we were older and independent, watching my dad move out made my mom freak out. It threw the family into a tailspin.

Rob and I lived with Mom at the house while Dad moved to a more single-friendly area called Long Beach where he got a one-bedroom apartment by the ocean and a red, convertible Fiat Spider. Clearly, he was going through a mid-life crisis. It was horrible in that house watching my mom fall apart, becoming angry and bitter. She was understandably hurt and increasingly difficult for me to deal with because I had no tolerance for it. I was a woman who now had a future, and she was a woman who had been left. It was not a good match.

After turning eighteen in March, I was working part-time in the local health food store and becoming even more educated about health and food. I read self-help books like *Diet for a Small Planet* by Frances Moore Lappe, *Dick Gregory's Natural Diet for Folks Who Eat: Cookin' With Mother Nature*, and *Heal Your Body* by Louise Hay. They were living a different life through their food choices. It gave me a new view of the world. It was those books that helped me control what I put into my mouth as well as taking care of my body. I was learning to control my mind as well.

A guy from high school named Frank came by the store one day that summer. He was a couple years older than I and already working on his career.

"Hey, Leslie, how are you?"

"I'm good," I said.

"I'm playing drums in this band now."

"That's cool."

"You used to sing with Noah's band. Are you still doing that?"

"No, we broke up."

"Oh, well, maybe you should come by and meet our band. Maybe you could do some backgrounds."

"What kind of band is it? What do you do?"

He told me a little about them and suggested I come by to meet everybody. When he mentioned where the rehearsal studio was, my heart lit up! He was talking about the same rehearsal studio I used to fantasize about, the one on Grand Avenue where I'd see the cool kids hanging out and smoking cigarettes.

My heart leapt, but I stayed cool. "I'd love to."

We set up a time and I drove to the meeting in my mother's dented Cutlass Supreme, "The Green Hornet," as we called it. I pulled up to the door and thought, *I gotta pop around to the back. There is no way I can let anyone see me get out of this shit box.* I was extremely anxious, but I knew that was where I wanted to be. I didn't know what to expect. I needed to make a good impression. It was like walking into a head shop. Arcade machines. Smoke wafting. Guitars on the walls. Guys everywhere. No women in sight. I immediately felt self-conscious. All eyes were on me and it was uncomfortable.

Frank walked over with his big smile and tight afro. "Come on, I'll take you downstairs to meet the guys." It was a long journey to descend the staircase to the A, B, and C rehearsal rooms. We stopped in one of them.

"Hi, my name is Linda," said the only girl I'd seen there. "I'm Dino's wife."

Then Frank said, "And this is Dino."

I immediately thought *Oh my God, I'm in love.* There he stood with a big, bright smile, black shiny hair, and dimples, like a cross between Steven Tyler and Joe Perry. Everything felt surreal. The band was called Felony, and the bass player, Mike, was even hotter with his tank top and military style cargo pants. Random thoughts were running through my head. *I'm not pretty enough. I'm too fat. I don't belong here.*

With his big smile, Dino said, "Hi, we write all of our own music. This is an original band. Come on, let's see what you can do."

Is this an audition? I was nervous, but after I sang a little, he asked if I'd like to join the band. It was like being asked to marry someone I was in love with. I said yes, of course. I will marry you! I will join your band! I knew this was it.

Over the next few months, they never gave me a lot of parts to sing because Dino was clearly the lead singer, but he would encourage me to join him on melodies and harmonies. It became a training ground for me. I started to find my place in the band and learned more each day. After that, I knew where I was going two days a week, three days when we had a show. I felt like I was finally moving in the right direction. Even if I didn't always feel confident, I knew that my voice would come through. I was a sponge. I watched and learned, taking in everything around me. I was a sensorial mess, but a great mess. I loved being in the studio making and recording music. I learned how to find my own sound, and I was encouraged to push myself even more. There were five members and bands are tough, like another family. There are strong male egos involved because somebody always wants to be on top. I was used to that with brothers and a father. That was ok. I didn't need to be on top. I was soaking it all up.

During the day I kept busy at the health food store, then we'd rehearse during the week and play gigs on the weekend if we were lucky. I learned how to be in front of an audience and dress for the stage. Mostly, I learned how to navigate around the dynamic of five confident, talented men. These guys wanted me to succeed because it made them sound better. Not too much though, I found out later. Mike and Dino took an interest in me and I'd learn more from them in private lessons away from the band. I learned a few other things as well. I was literally finding my voice, and it might not have felt natural at first, but it didn't take long. I was right where I was supposed to be, where preparation and opportunity meet.

After about a year, we had performed in multiple showcases and cut demo after demo, and my position in the band never seemed to elevate. I was still in the background with just a couple of shared lead vocals. What was changing was my confidence as a performer. I was dealing with their sexual advances, which was fine by me because they were all hot. They were having sword fights, but I was benefitting from it. However, I knew my time with the band was coming to an end because we weren't landing a record deal and egos were getting in the way.

During my first year of college, I couldn't stay with my mom any longer, so I sat down with my dad and said, "Hey, can I live with you?"

He said, "We can try it out, but it's a longer drive for you. Let's give it a couple of months." He got me a rollaway cot that I had to pack up and put in the closet during the day. He was into dating, being single, and having his freedom. Who was I to say no? I just made sure I was out of the house most nights either rehearsing with the band or on a date.

It was during that time that I met Ken in a local bar. I knew him through a mutual friend of ours. He was twenty years old and dated one of my friends. He was hot, he had a steady job, and he had money. He was sweet and loving and our relationship grew quickly. Soon I asked my dad if I could move in with Ken.

He said, "I want you to stay in college."

"Stay in college?"

"Try living on campus for a year first. I'll give you $200 a month."

To satisfy my father, I went to another Long Island university, C.W. Post.

Dad said, "If that doesn't work, then you can live with Ken."

"Really?"

"Just try it."

My anxiety once again increased as I had to move from my father's apartment to the dorm room. I took Ken to my dorm room every night. That lasted about three weeks. I couldn't believe my poor roommate was willing to put up with that shit. My parents were still trying to control what I should do.

I scoured the *Village Voice* classifieds every week looking for my next band. By that point I felt like I had a lot more experience on stage. I'd put the time in and paid my dues with Felony. Yet inside, those internal demons were still racking me with fear and anxiety.

Living in that dorm for a month scared me enough that I knew I had to feel secure, and Ken became what I later learned in behavior medication was a "safety zone" for me. He was willing to drive me everywhere. He took me to rehearsals, and anywhere else I needed to go. He was my savior. I barely lasted a semester at CW Post before moving in with Ken. I also continued my weekly operatic training with my coach and mentor, Maestro Gabor Carelli. I'd meet him at his apartment in the Dakota Building in New York for practice, and then audition for new bands.

Soon, I auditioned for a band I'd found called The Next. The guy was based out of White Plains, NY, and when I got there I saw that he was living in the carriage house next to a mansion. A Harvard alum just out of music school, he was a writer with some great songs. I knew that instinctually this was a good place to put my energy. I wouldn't be singing backgrounds anymore, and suddenly my career was heating up. I was officially part of The Next singing original, cutting edge "New Wave" music. Soon, I was rehearsing two or three days a week in White Plains and playing clubs in New York City. I was building a name for myself and the band. We were playing places like CBGBs, Gildersleeves, The Bitter End, and The Bottom Line. Finally, I was the lead singer, and Ken was always by my side.

It was during this time that my mom couldn't stand being in the house any longer without my father. She made a radical move to live at an ashram in Lenox, Massachusetts. She went to live a life of austerity and study under a guru with other disciples. Her plan was to study for a couple of months to learn who she was, to grow into who she wanted to become. She stayed for four years.

After she was there for about a year, my dad started becoming quite interested in her again. He said, "You need to go see your mother up there."

"What?" I was fully occupied with my own life.

"I think she's joined the Moonies."

"Why?"

"I think she's part of a cult," he added.

"You've gotta be kidding."

"Have your younger brother go with you when he's home for a school break."

"Fine, Dad."

Rob came home from college one weekend so that he and I could drive my mother's Camaro up to Massachusetts. The ashram was located just beyond the New York border and near the historic Tanglewood theatre that is famous for its music schools, high-profile performances, and Broadway-caliber productions. Once we arrived, I saw that our mother was living at an idyllic retreat of at least 75 tranquil acres. Rob and I were given private rooms where we could stay on the property and learn more about the facility. At first, when I saw that she was sharing a room with twenty other women and sleeping on a gym mat I said, "Mom, what the hell?"

Then I realized she was in a safe place, a haven for prayer and devoting herself to a life of inner peace and learning. I felt like she had found her sanctuary. Every day she woke up to natural, wholesome meals where the group ate together in silence. Then she would go to yoga and chanting classes. She was gradually changing herself. For her, it was a lifestyle. She was there to heal. I could feel that and so could Rob. I even joined some classes to spend time with her, and I started to see the benefits as well.

They encouraged family members to come and visit, and the first time I truly experienced peace was when doing some of the kundalini yoga and other courses. My mom was considered a disciple and even had an Indian Sanskrit name, Archer. Mom told me they had classes that would help with my emotional imbalance, the fears and anxieties I was struggling with. She was right. The yoga helped me slow down my breathing. The meditation helped control my thoughts and release the toxins in my system. Gradually, I felt more in control of my irrational fears. In fact, my mom was the first to help me put a word to my anxiety, which was agoraphobia, a fear of open spaces. That made sense after I'd had that attack without being inebriated and my fear of not being with a "safe" person. I learned that agoraphobics are usually people who need to stay in a calculated, comfortable area and always need to know where they are going because the fear of losing control is so great.

I appreciated my mom for opening up this world for me and my brother. I could build my mental "tool chest," but I couldn't live there like she did. So, she recommended a treatment center for me to help with my panic attacks since I had to go back and forth to New York for performances. I'm sure it was tough on Ken although he never complained. I knew I couldn't be a rock star and achieve the success I wanted if I couldn't even drive across the White Stone Bridge or get on a plane by myself. I needed to get healthy and emotionally strong to manage the fears that threatened my dream career.

I went to a behavior modification treatment center that specialized in agoraphobia and panic attacks. Between the meditation, therapy, and going to the inpatient program at the treatment center twice a week, I learned that I could control the panic. I learned how to breathe through the attacks, reprogramming my neurology one step at a time. I physically put myself in situations that I thought I'd never be able to do again. A counselor would walk and talk me through some of the places that typically would trigger my attacks like going by each of the exits on the parkway or driving closer and closer to a bridge that I couldn't previously cross without Ken. Now, working with her, and using tools like a simple rubber band on my wrist, helped me stop myself before escalating into a full-blown panic attack, no matter how many times I had to snap that band.

She would take me on the train and we'd get off at every stop and then wait to get back on. It was a mental exercise. It was work, just like I'd done to build muscle memory for my voice. This was the same thing. I needed to build my mental muscles to stop negative thoughts from getting out of control. The behavior modification helped me reframe my thoughts in a positive way to understand that this would not kill me.

Day after day, week after week, month after month, I was healing. When my thirteen-week program ended, I decided to continue with group therapy for another year. It was helpful talking with others who suffered from debilitating panic attacks. It took years to overcome my anxiety—to the extent that I have. I learned how to extend my freedom inch by inch, block by block; I earned my freedom. I chipped my way out of that lonely black canyon. Even now there are nights when I hear it barking at me like a junkyard dog, but I force myself to see it for what it is: a bark not a bite. Still, I will never forget just how dark and deep and close to the edge I got.

THE NEXT WAS STARTING to generate good buzz in the city. I was finding my way and gaining notoriety as a singer. We had two very close major record deals, a couple of demo parties, and several industry showcases. I was working hard and keeping my fears under control. Being part of any band is a lot of work. I was at the mercy of the leader, and the emotional needs of five different people. Just like with Felony, members of The Next started making decisions that I had no say in. It was their band, so it was their way or the highway. I felt like I needed to be the leader of my own destiny, and I needed to prove that to myself.

I was now able to drive over parkways and bridges to my own rehearsals. I no longer needed a safety zone. I had to prepare myself for the future, for *my* future. It was difficult, but I forced myself to pull away from Ken and the tender moments of sleeping in the same bed with him. I gradually moved into a separate room to ease the transition. It was the only way for me to heal and grow. Ken had provided me with so much security, but we both knew it was time. I loved him, but I needed to leave him.

At twenty, I moved back into the family home on California Avenue, but I was determined to keep myself on track and focus on my health. And with two bands under my belt, I was ready to go out on my own. I no longer wanted to be part of a band.

I was ready to be a solo artist.

# CHAPTER 3
## The White Russian

"SPITTLE, are you up?"

The voice startles me awake. Then I realize I'm back in the family house lying on my bed and staring at the ceiling I vowed I'd never look at again.

"Spittle, I need to talk to you."

Hugh is living in the dungeon—I mean basement. He calls me Spittle because I used to suck on my doll. I call him Spewey for some reason. Maybe because it rhymes with Hughie?

"You need to work," he says. "We have bills to pay!"

I look up to see Hugh standing in the doorway wearing his ever-present red plaid Scotchgard-looking robe and holding a stack of bills. "What do you suggest, Spew?" I ask.

"I have a gig for you."

"Yeah, what is it?"

"How does $25 an hour sound?" How does it sound? It sounded like I'd hit the jackpot.

"What do I have to do?" I asked as I looked at the unwashed mass of hair sticking up on his head and five days of facial stubble.

"Sing at a club."

"I don't do covers. I do original music."

"Well, you need to eat, don't you? And you sure as shit need to pay some of the bills around here. It's at a club in Brighton Beach called Odessa."

"Odessa? What does that even mean?"

"It's a Russian club. You sing from 9:00 to midnight and you make $25 an hour."

"How many nights?"

"Friday, Saturday, and Sunday."

It was an offer I couldn't refuse. Hugh set up a meeting for me, and I drove to the club in my beat-up, sky blue Datsun B210. I watched as the passing landscape changed from quaint houses and lush tress to apartment buildings and convenience stores. I passed under the Brighton Beach subway trestle and pulled into the parking lot of The Odessa Restaurant and Nightclub. I was definitely far away from my Long Island comfort zone.

I spoke to the two owners who were difficult to understand through broken English, but they had big smiles, were very passionate about music, and wore suits. It seemed legit, and I was hired on the spot to sing from 9:00 to midnight for $25 an hour.

Then one of them said, "Can you sing American Top 40?"

I'm gonna kill my brother! "Yes, I can." I checked out the club and saw that it had a surprisingly large stage complete with an eight-piece band of grown men, experienced musicians. They were serious about their entertainment. It was the real deal.

I arrived on a Friday at 8:30 for my first day of work. One of the owners greeted me. "Let me show you where to get ready," he said. We walked downstairs, and he pointed to the coat room. "There. You change there and then go upstairs to the stage."

He disappeared down the hall. I tapped lightly on the door and went in. There was a tall, gorgeous African-American woman standing there.

"Hi," she said. "You must be the new girl. This is where you get ready."

"Yeah, that's what I heard, but come on, a coat room? There's no dressing room?" I asked.

"No, this is it, but you won't be in here much, though."

"Really? Why not?"

"Because you're always on stage. You might get one break a night if you're lucky," she said. "Come on."

As I followed her up the stairs, she waved and hugged everyone we passed. Then she looked back at me and continued talking. "I'll give you the grand tour." She pointed to the back of the stage. "When you do get a break, you can sit on one of those stools." Someone came over and gave her a highball glass filled with brown liquid. She said something to him in Russian and then smiled at me. "They'll bring you these all night. It's cognac. It helps."

I thought, *What has Hugh gotten me into?* I'd only recently come out of behavior modification, and now I would be drinking all night? It was a tug of war in my head, but the bottom line was that I needed the money. I said, "By the way, I'm Leslie."

"Hi, Leslie. I'm Terri. Terri Rojers."

She made her way to the stage and began singing in Russian, flashing her wide smile. It felt like I was in another world, and I guess I was. She resembled Diana Ross in her fancy gown with flowing hair and long legs. I felt out of place with my punky clothes and spiked hair. When I got on stage, I followed her lead, and did the best I could to keep up. It was trial by fire. I was learning on the job. The band members called me "Lucia."

Boris would hold his trumpet in one hand and toss the microphone to Terri. "Get up there and do 'I'm So Excited.'" Whenever Terri would start singing, the crowd would go crazy. They would jump out of their seats and dance in front of the stage, yelling out more song requests.

When 12:00 rolled around, I told the guys, "Ok, well, it's time for me to head out." They all stared. Then Terri came over.

"We stay as long as the band is playing, and they play as long as we are being paid. We can sometimes make several hundred a night."

"I was only hired for three hours a night," I said. "My shift is done." That worked for a few nights, but by the second week, my new coworkers weren't going to let me leave before them. "But I don't know any of these songs," I said.

"Don't worry," said Terri. "Just watch me."

Boris said, "Lucia, you will come to my house during the day next week and learn the songs." His delivery was a mix between Arnold Schwarzenegger and my drill sergeant teacher Mrs. Davies.

I turned to Terri, "Are you kidding me? I have to learn these songs in Russian?"

"Yeah, it's not too hard. I did it when I first started."

"Really?" I said. "How long have you been here?"

"Three years."

Wow. That seemed like a lifetime to me. I drove home thinking, *I'm gonna kill Hughie.* First, I find out I have to stay all night long and on top of that I have to learn Russian on my own time? And I have to change in a coat room? This is not what I had in mind.

When I got home, Hughie said, "Remember, I'm just like an agent. I get 10% of everything you make."

"Fine." I didn't have the energy to argue. I'd leave his money at the top of the dungeon/basement stairs, never descending into his cave.

Working at The Odessa was like seeing a car wreck. I couldn't help but watch the craziness that went on night after night. It wasn't what I'd imagined for my music career, but I didn't have a lot of options. At first, I wasn't able to share in the tips that were collected. "No, Lucia," Boris said. "When you spend more time with the band, you will get your cut." I couldn't catch a break. Still, I went back weekend after weekend and learned from the school of hard knocks. It was an amazing training ground, because I had to perform songs outside of my comfort zone, and I had to do them in English and Russian.

Fortunately, I had an amazing teacher in Miss Terri Rojers. I watched how she worked with the band and sang to the crowd as they cheered "Terri! Terri!" I learned things I would have never been exposed to otherwise. Singing Top 40 songs was something I never thought I'd be doing, but with Terri's support, I was soon working the stage like a pro. It was much different from being part of a band, and I had to remember that. I was used to writing original music, creating my art. This was on another level. I was there to entertain. It was a different skill set, and the experience helped me grow even more as a performer.

Terri and I became fast friends. There were plenty of differences, but we shared a love of music. She was from Long Island as well, but she lived in Hampstead. I found out she was thirty and had two children. The oldest was twelve. I had no idea. She said, "I stay here three days a week with my friend and when I'm not working, I go home to my two girls who stay with my mother." It was a different way of life from what I knew. She was already a mother, but I respected her hustle and the dedication to her children.

As Malcolm Gladwell writes in his book *Outliers*, 10,000 hours of soul-wrenching hard work is the secret behind any "overnight success." The Odessa is where I put in many of those hours to perfect my art. I was working night after night for an audience that loved music almost as much as the endless bottles of vodka and cognac.

After about a month of work, I stood at the top of the stairs and yelled down to Hughie, "Spew-boy, this is the last $30 you're ever going to get from me. It's craziness over there! I am basically working for the mob. I'm in little Russia," I screamed into the dungeon. "I might as well be in St. Petersburg. I'm on a bread line. I'm there till five. I deserve every dollar I make. We're done. Your final agency fee is here on the top of the steps. Don't ever ask me for a nickel more."

Just like that I had fired my first agent, but I did have a job. Each night, I never knew if there was going to be a fight or if someone was going to pull out a gun. It was completely unpredictable. There were lots of weddings that took place day and night. Fathers would be yelling at daughters, marrying them off to gypsies, and throwing the band $1,000 a song. Math is not my strong suit, but I learned fast how to calculate what my cut of that would be.

Terri would come to work wearing some beautiful jewelry, something new almost every week. "Is that costume?" I asked.

"Oh, no, it's a gift from Boris."

Soon, I was called "The White Russian" and Terri was "The Black Russian." She was well-respected and quite powerful. She even got her own stool for breaks. It also helped that she dated some of the big bosses at the club. Every night, she dazzled me and the crowd with her beautiful clothes, her amazing memory for songs, and her fearlessness on the stage. She was always smiling, and everybody loved her. She was a shining star. Vocally, we were different. I was much more trained and precise, but what she lacked in technical ability she made up for with personality. She could sell it, and that was what the audience responded to. She was one of a kind, and I loved being with her.

In order to stay, I had to learn Russian. Terri went with me to Boris's apartment and helped me practice. I learned the curse words first because, believe me, they came in handy. I paid attention to the clientele and I'd never seen anything like it. Women came in like they were walking a fashion runway. Some were as young as eighteen, and some much older. They all wore so much makeup it was never easy to tell them apart.

I always tried to park as close to the entrance as possible because I did not want to hang around in the parking lot. One night, I had to park far away. I saw a car out front with multiple police cruisers around it, blood everywhere, and a shattered windshield. I went inside and looked around. "Terri, what's going on out there?"

She said, "Oh, there was a shooting."

"No kidding. That Oldsmobile is messed up. Was someone shot? What happened?"

"Who knows?" she shrugged. "I think someone died."

I mentioned during one of my breaks that I needed a car. My Datsun was on its last few miles. Terri suggested that we drive over to New Jersey the next weekend and look around. "They have some good tax breaks," she said.

Later, we were in the parking lot when one of the guys from the club came up to me and said, "Lucia, I got a nice car for you."

"You do?"

"Oh yeah, an Oldsmobile. Beautiful car. I'll give you a good price."

"Where is it?"

He said, "We park it out back."

I look over and it's the same car that I saw with the blood and the broken windshield. "Is that the car that had the bullet holes?"

"No, no. We fix it. Everything fixed. All clean. We'll give you good price."

"Are you crazy? No, that's bad juju. I'm okay. Thank you so much."

The Russians threw around a lot of cash and lived hard. Terri and I were in the middle of the mayhem, and we saw a lot of the nefarious activity. We kept our mouths shut and our heads down as we walked through the crowd, and turned on the smiles when we hit the stage.

I had a Russian boyfriend who traveled to Europe every other month. He seemed so refined and classy to me with his nice car and fancy clothes. He turned me on to fashion and I started learning about high-end designers like Gautier, Versace, and Thierry Mugler. He had a townhouse in Sheepshead Bay with a disco in the basement and a sauna that he used to purge himself of the alcohol he'd drank the night before. It was unbelievable. He'd just go sweat it out. Through him, I learned so much about fashion, culture, jewelry, and food.

In fact, the style from my first video, "Tell It to My Heart," was what I called glam/goth, a mashup of the fancy Russian influence of designer labels and the punk vibe of places I visited around 2nd Avenue and St. Mark's Place in Greenwich Village. That was the epicenter of counterculture with bars like the Cat Club and CBGBs and punk stores like Trash & Vaudeville and Nasty Habits. The Russian Boyfriend didn't care much for my look and called me "Punky Schmunky," so my goth/glam style was a good compromise.

Going to Odessa each weekend was becoming less and less glamorous. At the beginning of the night, beautiful Russian women would come in dripping in jewels and men in the latest fashions, yet underneath that beauty and glamor was a lot of darkness, brutality, and violence. When the lights came up at 5:00 or 6:00 in the morning, reality set in. It looked like the aftermath of a war. Broken bottles. Stacks of dirty dishes. It was easy to get caught up in the glitz and glamour at the start of the evening, but all I really cared about was the tip jar. I hung in there. I needed the money to finance my dreams. Cash was always flowing, but so were the bad things. Where there's too much good, there's often evil.

As far as my solo career, I had put it on hold so that I could support myself financially. Now it was time. I needed to get back to my dream. It was imperative for me to send out demos and get into the studio with a producer who would understand me. I'd been in two bands already. I knew what it took to work with a producer and make music and write songs. A solo artist is what I had set my sights on. No longer would I be in a band unless it had my name on it.

KISS FM 102.7 WAS A breaking radio station in New York playing artists like Sade, Madonna, and Gwen Guthrie. There was also another exciting station called KTU that played dance, house, and club hits. It was intriguing to hear these urban sounds mixed with pop. I knew music was changing, especially when I heard singers like Anita Baker, and especially Aretha Franklin's "Who's Zoomin' Who?" That was a career comeback for her and a sign that artists with big voices were moving into the pop genre. Then there was a girl from New Jersey named Whitney Houston with an album called *How Will I Know?* That song perfectly bridged the gap between pop and R&B. I was hooked. That was what I wanted to be singing. Whoever was putting out that music really understood how to take advantage of women with big voices.

My phone rang one day.

"Hey, it's Frank," said the drummer from Felony who had become a good friend.

"Hey, how are you doing?"

"Great. Who are you singing with now?"

"I'm in between. Working on going solo."

"Ok, I have a guy you should meet."

"Who is it?" I asked.

"A music producer, a young guy. Are you still sending out demos?"

"Yes."

"Great. If you can give me a cassette, I'll get it to him."

I was still answering ads in *The Village Voice* just like in the movie *Desperately Seeking Susan*, but I was desperately seeking a new single. I found an ad that sounded interesting and went in to meet the British producer with a label called Jive Records. I did the demo on it for them, and they called me back twice.

Soon I got another call and it was a guy with a British accent. I thought he was from the audition I'd done, and I was sure I'd gotten the gig. "My name is Ric. Frank gave me your demo."

What are the chances there would be another British producer? "Hi, how's it going?"

"Great," he said. "I want to try you out on a track I'm working on. Have you heard of a song called 'All Night Passion' by Alicia?"

"Of course," I told him. "I love that song."

"I worked on the engineering. I'm working on some other stuff in a studio in Belmont."

"Really?"

He said, "I love your voice."

"You love my voice?"

"Yes, I do."

That's how I met aspiring music producer Ric Wake. When I went to see him at the studio, I saw a nineteen-year-old with a football player build and messy blond hair living like a squatter in the basement with his friend and business partner Dave. They were young kids who looked like they needed clothes, food, and maybe some sunshine. They were living and breathing music as they worked in that recording studio. Ric had a big smile and he was encouraging and easygoing.

He said, "You're an amazing singer and I really want to work with you. Let's find some music!"

We established a good rapport and got right to work. Sometimes I felt like the sugar mama, because I'd come in straight from the club with cash in hand. We'd go out, get some food, sometimes new clothes, and then head back to the studio. The owner had them working down there like it was a sweatshop, but they didn't seem to mind. They'd sleep all day and work all night.

Rick was as hungry, if not as crazy, as I was. We had the same drive and ambition and we propelled each other to build the dream. We were quite the pair. I'd found my musical soulmate. The other song that I had tried out for with Jive Records was called "Touch Me" and it became a hit for an up-and-coming singer named Samantha Fox, a "Page Six Girl" from *The Sun*.

I'd already played some of the biggest clubs in New York City, and I had paid my dues. I had been practicing, molding, fine-tuning, and discovering everything about my voice—every mistake, every nuance. When you love something so much and become passionate about it, it consumes you, as my voice did for me. It became a tool for me to express myself. It's no different than an athlete, designer, or doctor. From a seed to a nurtured skill, I believe people are innately born with a gift, something unique to them. It's the hours of work and muscle-building and perseverance that takes someone from good to great. I pushed through. It was mind over matter.

During that time, despite the attention and accolades, I never felt beautiful, but I knew I was special. That was a struggle for me. I never looked in the mirror and said, *Oh my God, you're gorgeous.* But with sheer determination, I felt I could be beautiful. I knew I had a gift, so I focused on that and thought the rest would come. *I'm going to be beautiful. I am someone you're going to have to look at. I am going to demand attention and I'll get it because I earned it.*

Ric said, "Guess who I met. Dee Snider."

"Dee Snider? He went to my high school. They're massive now." I'd seen Twisted Sister in the clubs for years and was amazed at how they put on makeup and crazy clothes and soon they were all over MTV yelling, "We're Not Gonna Take It." Videos were perfect for their image, and they blew up. I was very proud because "Strong Island" stands by their own.

When Ric said that Dee wanted to meet me and that he was into what we were doing, I said, "That's amazing. I'd love that." It was inspiring to meet someone who had "made it," and I was ready for my turn.

Ric and I knew we needed a song. *The* song. Twelve-inch vinyl records were popular, and singles were being released right and left. Tommy Boy, Zomba, and Jive record companies were growing their list of artists. The way to get played on the radio was to release a 12" single of one song. Getting that single added to the playlist of one of the late-night mix shows could generate enough call-in interest that the radio station would take notice and start pushing the song. I just needed to find the right one for me. Ric and I were attached to Joey's independent record label, and I was packaged as the artist "Les Lee."

Many mornings at 4:00 a.m., I'd finish at the Odessa club in Brooklyn and drive on the BQE and Belt parkways singing the *Twilight Zone* theme song in my head. I was leaving Terri Rojers, Russian mobsters, and all kinds of excess to retreat into the bowels of a dark studio where I would find so much comfort. I was able to spend the next seventy-two hours with my people doing what I loved. It was through Ric and the others coming into the studio that we started building relationships with writers, producers, and even singers from all over the area including Trenton gospel and church groups. We were making great music.

It was fun, but this was a business. Drop a 12", throw it against the wall, and see if it sticks. The owner of the studio was caught up in our dedication and the time we were putting in. We were making songs and printing vinyl that Joey would release in hopes that it would get picked up by radio. This was where I put in the work. This was my internship. From the nights spent singing in the nightclub to the hours watching producers and programmers making records, I was studying how to become an artist, developing my ear for music, and creating my own sound. It was so cool that I could finally say I was a solo artist. Ric was my producer and we were partners. We were building our perfect wall of sound, and nobody was going to stop us. We were best of friends and loved each other. He believed in me and I believed in him.

When anyone came to the studio to make a record, Ric would make sure to get me involved. If it was a demo session, I'd do the backgrounds for people like Billy T. Scott and Jamillah. Billy could arrange vocals like no one I'd ever heard. He would come in with his Jheri curl and soft-spoken voice, but when he sang it was like nothing I'd ever heard. He had a three- or four-octave range. (He later worked on Mariah Carey's first album and many others.) Ric and I were a team and we named our company Bleux Productions. At the time, we called that music "hip-hop," which later became known as "freestyle." It was the 133 beats per minute (BPM) style of music that was burning up The Bronx, Brooklyn, and soon Miami and the rest of the country. A music genre was fast emerging. We were very encouraged by the response from the two 12" records I released under the name Les Lee. One was called "I'm the One You Want." (I still have some of the original records. A collector's item.) That song had decent crossover and got a good response in the clubs and with promoters, but still it wasn't "the one."

Ric was also working on other music and one of the acts, Private Possession featuring singer Hunter Hayes, blew up and they were signed to Tommy Boy Records on the strength of a 12" single called "Are You Wid It?" with me doing backgrounds. That was the biggest thrill of my life because I was part of it, and we were starting to get radio attention. Ric said, "We need a song for you, something that can cross over. Hunter's song is great, but it's not going to fully cross over. We need a record that can go from the clubs to the music charts. And we need to finance it ourselves."

"How much money do you think we need to do that?" I asked. "Do we even have a song?" I knew that Ric had an ear and could hear a song's potential when no one else could. More than that, I trusted and believed in him. We were making some traction. We'd sit downstairs coming up with ideas and then go upstairs to create the songs. While he was focused on the concepts, I was the practical one. I wanted to know what it would cost and what I had to do to make it happen.

That next week, I had left the Odessa at 4:00 a.m. and dropped Terri off at her apartment. As I was driving slowly on the Westside highway, I saw a guy I'd gone to high school with named Anthony. I pulled over and we started talking. Before cell phones or emails, that's how we did it. We'd see a friend and pull over to catch up. He told me he was working in music at Warner Chappell Publishing. I thought that was an amazing coincidence, and I was always on the hustle. "I've been doing some 12" records and I really need the right single."

"Get in touch with Mary Ann. She works with me," he said, giving me his card. "She might be able to help."

The next day, I called Mary Ann and asked if she could send us some material to listen to. I told her I was new to this and wasn't sure how it worked.

She said, "I am happy to help. Any friend of Anthony's is a friend of mine."

Soon, a demo cassette tape came in the mail with song titles handwritten on the label. It had eight tunes on it. I had saved up enough money to move into a small apartment, and Ric and I were in my living room listening to each song carefully. As we played each one, I watched him to get his reaction.

Finally, he stopped the cassette and said, "This is the song we should do."

"This is *the* song?" I asked. I read the label. "'Tell It to My Heart?'"

"Yes, this is the one." He was firm on that song and said we should use my voice to its fullest, not tone it down or hold back. "This song will support your vocals melodically and vocally, and I like the lyrics. We need to be in control of it."

I said, "Let me ask my dad if we can borrow the money."

Ric and I met with my father in the kitchen at our family house. We were seated at the round antique dining table with claw feet that had been partially stripped in a half-hearted attempt to refinish it.

"How much are we talking?" asked Jack Wunderman. He had been watching me work for the last several years, going from one band to another and then singing solo in the clubs. He would even come to shows when he could. So, he knew that I had been working hard on my music and had never asked him for anything. He believed in me and wanted to help.

We pitched him with a business plan and asked him to loan us the $6,000 we needed to produce, mix, record, and master a single. *The* single.

My dad said, "Are you willing to sign a contract?"

"Yes," I said. "We promise to pay all of it back."

"I'll have my secretary, Betty, type one up." We soon had the one-page, typed contract in hand. Ric and I signed it immediately. (I have it in my office today.)

Ric wanted to take the money we had borrowed and record the song at another studio up in Glen Cove, NY called Cove City Sound. It was owned by Richie Cannata (Billy Joel's sax player) and his business partner Clay. Dee Snider was working there producing a female group during his off time from Twisted Sister. We had seen how the other independent records had done and we wanted to make sure this song was handled differently. We went there with $6,000 and never looked back.

In 1986, with all the pieces in place—the song to record, the producer, the musicians—I went to the studio every day after working all night at Odessa. I was doing the vocals for the song at 5:00 a.m. with Bob Cadway, one of the greatest vocal engineers and guitar players I have ever worked with. He was my vocal engineer for years, and he could do wonders with a reel-to-reel. Ric, Bob, and I worked hard to stack the vocals. I'd do six or seven takes, add in the harmonies, then fine-tune the vocals for several hours with the precision of a mathematical equation.

"Go back in there. You can do it better," Bob would encourage me. Ric would spend days just on perfecting the snare, kick drum, and base lines. I would draw graphs of the song on several pieces of paper. Mapping it out. Then I'd add the lyrics to show how each word should be phrased. I would shuffle them around and make changes on the fly, based on rehearsals. We were consumed with a common goal. When the song was finally done, we sat back and listened to it. Ric said it was ready.

We were passed over by Atlantic Records, Tommy Boy, and several other companies that Ric had taken it to. After being rejected from the big labels, we decided to put it out on our own.

We would get it on the midnight shows and then the local radio stations. That was our plan. We went to Burt, one of the top record promoters in the city, since we'd worked with him in the past. He was going to help us get the word out about the new single.

Soon we got a call from him. "Hey, I got some interesting news and I want to talk to you two about it." We went into his office and Burt said, "I got a call from a guy over at Arista Records. He works in A&R. I sent the song over there."

I said, "I thought we were planning on our own release."

"Well, apparently they want to buy the single."

"What?" I said.

"Yeah, Arista Records wants to do a deal on the single with you and Bleux Productions."

I asked, "Who is Arista Records?"

"They have artists like Whitney Houston and Aretha Franklin."

"Whoa, wait," I said. "The same label with those artists wants this record?"

It was like the song had made its way to Zeus on Mount Olympus. They were singers with big voices and they were doing what I knew I could do. Whoever was behind those singers understood the sound we were creating. That was a perfect example of manifesting my own destiny.

I told Ric we needed to take this offer seriously, and then the promoter interrupted. "I need to make a deal with both of you," he said, "because I am the one who took this to them." Hence, I was getting my first lesson in the music *business*. He wanted a finder's fee and a little bit more. He took points. That "introduction" would end up costing me for the rest of my professional career.

We ended up doing a deal with Arista Records that was called a "single, single, option album" contract. That meant they could drop me if the single didn't do well or they could have the option of another single and an album. It was an unusual arrangement, but still we couldn't believe our luck. This major label wanted our song. It was an incredible feeling.

We went back to the studio and I said to Ric, "Are we really going to put this out as Les Lee or Leslie Wunderman?" Those names didn't seem to me like a Whitney or Aretha. I was Leslie

Wunderman and I didn't believe in *her*, but I could believe in someone else. In fact, I wanted to be somebody else. I needed to create distance from Leslie and all the anxiety and pain she represented in order to blossom into that flower of freedom. I was ready to grab the carrot dangling in front of me and be the person I had always wanted to be. The artist. It was a smart business move because I'd been known as Les Lee on a couple of independent songs, but it was more than that. It was necessary in order for me to be the artist I wanted to be, somebody other than Leslie.

In one of our late-night studio sessions, I was doing background vocals for Dee, Ric, and a few other guys. We were still excited about the record deal. Dee said, "Girl, if you're going to change your name, it should be something cool like a guy's name. An androgynous one like Frankie or Nicky or Tommy."

Dee's engineer chimed in. "My girlfriend's name is Tommy. Actually, my real girlfriend's name is Taylor, but when I tell her I'm going out with Tommy she thinks I'm out with a guy."

We weren't paying attention to his story. Once he said "Taylor," we all looked at each other. Everyone loved that name, and at the time it was unusual. We decided to take a break and go next door to the bar. (There's always a bar within walking distance of a recording studio. Guaranteed.) Richie was having a baby, so we borrowed his book of baby names and went for a drink. Ric was drinking a friggin' Shirley Temple, and I was putting back a Vodka Soda. We took out the book and tried to find a name that went with Taylor. Finally, Ric pointed to a name.

"Dane."

I said, "Dane?"

"Yes," he said. "It sounds European. Danish."

"That's not quite my look, is it?" I asked.

He said, "I think it sounds very musical. I love the way it flows. Taylor Dane. That's what we should do."

"OK," I agreed. "That's what we will do."

We gave that name to the label and I was signed to my deal as Leslie Wunderman aka Taylor Dane. Within a few weeks, after some touchups on the mixes, the record company was ready to print the singles. That morning, I got a call from Hughie.

"Leslie, didn't you say something about using the name Taylor Dane?"

"Yeah, why?" Coming from him I knew it couldn't be good.

"Well, Sis, I think you have a problem. There's a porn star named Taylor Dane."

"What? No shit! People are going to think I'm a porn star?"

Sure enough, within an hour we got a call from Business Affairs at Arista Records. I couldn't believe that I'd picked a porn star name from a baby book. I didn't know what to do, so I said, "Maybe put a 'y' in there similar to the spelling of Taylor. Taylor Dayne." They went for it and everyone was happy that things were back on track. Now I wouldn't be thought of as a singing porn star! Thank God for Hughie.

In late 1986, with that settled, Arista went through with the deal that included the promoter (who wanted his introduction fee plus points) and an attorney. They paid us a whopping advance of $18,500 for the single "Tell It to My Heart," which I split with Ric after we paid my dad back for the loan. That left each of us with $6,250 and we had to pay Burt. The single was released in 1987 with a graphic orange sleeve that had my name spelled out in graffiti art. There was no picture of me. Just my name and the name of the song.

The label put the single out in Europe first and it started blowing up, chart by chart, country by country. It was spreading like wildfire. The record label demanded that I do promotion, and that I needed a photo shoot. I needed to do this. I needed to do that. Suddenly, I had to be everywhere at once. That's what "overnight success" is really like, working hard for years, and then working even harder.

Arista made several mistakes with me and that song. They had no images of me. They also had no video, and most importantly, there was no album to sell, just the single. They were losing a big opportunity to make even more money and they knew it. I was thrown into a whirlwind game of catch-up.

Soon, I was off to Europe on my first promotional tour behind a hit single. And true to my word, I took Terri Rojers with me.

# CHAPTER 4
## *Fame*

"**I**'M GONNA SHIT MYSELF, Joe! Seriously, right here and right now!" I'm speaking in hushed tones with rapid fire to anyone who will listen, but mostly to Joe Lennane, my tour manager. He just listens and smiles.

We're standing backstage at the arena in Barcelona, Spain and I'm being told it's time to take the stage. Somehow, I have to propel myself up a 30-foot-long aluminum ramp at a forty-degree angle. I can't move. My feet are planted, my stomach in knots, my bowels are knocking. All I hear is this deafening roar. The rumble of 60,000 fans together in one place screaming, shouting, yelling, overwhelmed with excitement for the show to begin. The ramp looks to me like a gangplank. A long walk to my death.

It's 1988 and this is the *Bad Tour*. The biggest tour of all time with the biggest artist in the world, Michael Jackson. Me, I'm the hottest, freshest, female artist to break out of the US and Europe over the last year. And to prove it, here I am opening up for The King of Pop in the largest stadium in the world.

"I'm gonna throw up, Joe!" I peek from the side of the stage and look out into the sea of people. How could all these people be here? How can Michael have so many fans? It seems impossible, definitely indescribable.

But the sound was far more deadly to me, the continuous roar in the coliseum. Never had I heard anything else like it. The sound of 10,000 hungry lions waiting for a meal.

And I'm it, the fresh meat being thrown to them. On the large MegaTron screens on the side of stage, I can see people screaming, miles of people crawling like ants, one on top of the other, often being hosed down as heat and exhaustion took over. The crowds. This was Michael Mania and hysteria in full effect. Arenas sold out throughout Europe. All to see the greatest artist of all time.

And here I am...

The little Jewish girl from New York. Still getting used to being called "Taylor," who four weeks earlier moved out of her rental apartment in Rockville Centre. The girl with two international hit records and a third single climbing the charts, opening up for the biggest star on the planet. This must be the sound gladiators heard as they were tossed into battle.

I continue ranting between breaths, yelling into Joe's ear. Sweat and fear dripping through my makeup and leather outfit, "Joe, are you fucking kidding me? There's no way I'm going out there! Look at all those people! They're gonna eat me!"

After so many years spent practicing, perfecting, working at my craft, dreaming of this moment. All the work I put in at endless gigs and shitty clubs, the years I spent healing and harnessing my panic attacks, learning how to manage my anxieties, I feel overwhelmed with joy and dread.

Joe continues to smile at me, and then yells over to the band, "You ready?" They nod yes to Joe but look like deer in headlights. Joe, the greatest tour manager I ever had and a dear friend, held my arm. Next to him Terri Rojers, my girl. Next to her Tommy Byrnes my rock and Frank D.; my people, my friends, my team side by side with me on this, ride or die.

One foot in front of the other, knowing it's now or never, I take a deep breath. Joe's hand gently pushes me forward as I hurl myself up the ramp and into the arms of the audience.

♭

*Tell It to My Heart* the album was released in 1988. I was internationally very famous by then, but back home in the States people were just getting to know who Taylor Dayne the artist was. I needed better promotion as an artist and the record company needed to sell records, not just singles. The "Overnight Stardom" was a myth, as I knew all the years I put in prior. "More" was what was needed. More promotional and more marketing campaigns to build the image of me as a legit artist, more photos, more images, more videos as more of my songs were released. The hits continued as I dominated the charts and broke records.

The record company, the corporate machine, was in overdrive now to catch up with the success of the first two singles and with developing me as a great artist, not a one-hit wonder. But most importantly selling records. Singles were nice, but let's not forget this is the music business and selling records *is* the business. Promoting, marketing, packaging, and artist imaging is paramount. Development began with building a glam squad of wardrobe, makeup, and hair stylists.

And my Glam Team worked hair extensions, crimping irons, black eyeliner, and red lipstick—incorporating the looks of the Russian girls and the club girls. Designer and street. Merging new wave/punk and glamour. The years I spent watching the parade of designer clothes to beat faces, from Odessa to St. Marks and 2nd Avenue, Love Spit Love, Danceteria, The Pyramid Club, Cat Club, and The Saint. Music and art and style merged. The iconic red lipstick on my plump, pouting lips the first image fans saw of me in *Tell It to My Heart* with crimped bangs became the forever ingrained image of Taylor Dayne.

The first video shoot for *Tell It to My Heart* was in a huge warehouse in Queens. Rehearsing and prepping for two days between promotional and radio shows. I had a choreographer and two dancers, no set really, just a loft space, dollies, cameras, white walls, makeup, a hair stylist, and two dancers.

My mound of crimped hair blowing effortlessly as floor fans were placed; my big lips locked dead into the camera lens. Heat and intensity. Capturing the moment. The song, the wall of sound Ric created of bass, bells, and balls influenced from the streets and clubs of New York.

I met with director Scott Kalvert at rehearsals, going over the concept with him. It was really a first for both of us as we talked with makeup and hair and wardrobe. We all went to work. The first collaborative experience I had with my image and professional stylists and I loved it. I knew how important image was, so I knew how important the director was. I learned how important lighting was. I watched and learned as these talented artists in fashion were imaginative and creative. I shared my personal ideas and style.

When I saw my final result, wow! The striking image looking back at me in the mirror. I was big. I was me, but I was bigger. In my Norma Kamali black bodysuit, bustier holding me all in, a black leather bomber jacket, and my own personal neoprene high-waisted skirt from Nasty Habits. The director said, "We don't need anything else, just you and the camera. You're enough." It was music to my ears.

*In 1988 a young woman of undiscernible ethnicity dominates the charts, the clubs, and MTV/VH1 in leather and lace, bold red lipstick, pouting lips.* "Powerful," "sexual," and "glamorous" were words used to describe me. As well as, was I black, white, Latina?

As the song blared loudly in the warehouse, I stared down the lens of that camera for sixteen hours. I listened, watched, learned, and absorbed take after take. At 2:00 a.m., I watched the final cuts of a girl walking barefoot in red paint. I know the energy I spent there and how exhilarated and exhausted I felt. Like I felt in the recording studio doing vocals or live on stage. Here I found another form of creativity that was fun and imaginative. As the hours ticked by, I was growing the muscle and stamina it would take to be a pop star. Effort and energy. Preparation meets opportunity.

People always comment to me, *your music is so passionate, your voice is So Big. You're so down to earth. You're so real, like you're in the same room with me when I hear you sing...* From my first introduction to the world, I can honestly say that passion has never left. It's the real deal. When I reach down deep into my soul to pull a note out, I want the listener to feel it, to know it. I want it to be delivered straight into their hearts.

I don't remember too many specific experiences from my early years of fame. It's more a blur of events. I was often so tired, running on fumes from plane to plane to radio stations, airports to stages, to Europe. But I will always remember the feeling of that initial fame and stardom.

A Pop/Rock/Glam Goddess was born. The video was released to mesmerized fans all over the world. Even myself. That girl looking fierce, powerful, and confident was groundbreaking, that image forever imprinted in the minds of every young girl and boy dancing their own trail into the night.

As the demands of my career grew, so did the record company's. I kept my promise to Terri Rojers—I took her with me when quitting Odessa for the final time a few months earlier. We had no weekly income other than what the record company doled out. We needed money to live on. I soon learned how upside-down this really can be.

I truly needed Terri. She was an integral part of my team and of my sanity, and now we were both in very similar financial positions. Mostly broke really, with financial responsibilities, her with two kids to support and me with growing crew members and attorneys to support. It was very clear that I needed management in place to manage me. But more importantly, I needed a buffer between me and the label. I needed a manager to help manage the record company. My days were filled with TV appearances, in-person radio interviews, in-store record appearances, press interviews on the phone or in person.

Anytime there was downtime, I was on a phone for a few hours of interviews in Europe or South Asia or Japan, in a hotel room, an airport, or somewhere in between. You could see me in many an airport digging out calling cards from the record company, on a payphone or in a lounge hunkered down for an hour or so between layover flights making calls for interviews and radio.

Terri was with me making memories every step of the way. We saw the Berlin wall up, and then we saw it come down. From Munich to London, Sweden to Italy, France to Spain. Whatever artists were at the top of the charts and playing on the radio our paths crossed. We were in the same hotels. We were in the same TV studios. We were in the same radio stations.

One memory I hold dear took place at one such TV taping in a studio two hours outside London. Having arrived hours before rehearsal and taping, jet lag not an option, I sat in my hotel room near the TV studio in the middle of rural nowhere. I heard from my record rep some rumblings about who else was taping with me. Billy Ocean was one of the artists. And then she said, "Get this, and Robert Plant." Stop my beating heart. BS. She was like, "Nope, he's on a solo press tour of his new album and is supposed to be on the show." I was buzzing, but mostly I was jet-lagged and went to get a couple hours sleep before they called me in for makeup, hair, and rehearsal.

When we got to the studio, we went directly into very needed makeup and hair. As I walked into the room with Miss Terri Rojers, several chairs had people in them. We couldn't see any faces just backs of heads. As I sat in my assigned chair, I began studying the heads of hair in the mirror. I couldn't make out any faces, but one particular mop stood out, like a halo of blond curls. As I turned my chair around discreetly to see better, I heard a merry voice with an English accent laugh out loud and continue on with his story, all while acting out the tale in one hand and sipping a can of beer held in the other. It was 10 a.m. *Dear God, tell me this is real!*

When Mr. Charming eventually stood up, all 6 feet 2 inches of him in black leather jacket, jeans and a smile built of swagger, in all his glory was the one and only Robert Plant. The room stopped. I know I stopped breathing. As I studied him in the mirror, he noticed me and when he walked over to my chair, Terri was looking at me in disbelief.

Robert said, "Hello, Love. My band mates say I should come and watch you perform at rehearsal."

I was speechless. Robert was tall, beautiful, and well spoken, but really, he was fucking Robert Plant. I was in full-blown fan attack. And more amazingly, Mr. Plant was clearly flirting with me. I still remember exactly what I was wearing and of course, the infamous photo of him and me on the cover of *The Sun* is for forever. My smile and excitement all captured in the swept-off-my-feet photo. My hair, lips, red plaid Gaultier jacket and leather Alaia skirt in all its glory. Rock n' roll indeed.

Robert continued to charm his way right into my ears as he laughed and joked and talked and snake-charmed me all the way down the hall to the set. Then he put his hand on my neck and shoulders, gently massaging me and testing out the foreplay waters as he whispered things into my ear all the way to set for blocking. I turned around to Terri who was all legs walking behind me with a grin from ear to ear. Taking it all in, the record rep's mouth dropped wide open in shock.

Soon Billy Ocean, not one to be left out of the fun, caught up to Miss Jones, not missing a chance to get his flirt on with her.

Robert wooing me, "Where are you staying? What hotel are you at? Come stay with me tonight."

I'm trying to put two words together, but I'm all tongue-tied. And then his hands are on my neck and my shoulders! He's touching me!! In my head *OMG! Hell, yes! I'm staying right here with Robert Plant.*

It was when I looked over his shoulder that I saw the look of "Hell No" on my record rep Doe's face, giving me a SMH look and mouthing one word. *No...* I'm like No??? What!! This is Robert Plant. This can't be happening!

Terri eventually had to intervene. "Tay, there's a private plane waiting to take us back to London for the BRIT awards. Remember, honey? You're nominated for Female Artist of the Year. You *have* to go."

My heart was sinking. Robert kept on talking and all I wanted to do was stay in the arms of Robert Plant. I wanted to be that girl. The girl in *Rolling Stone* magazine. Why can't I have that...a night like one of those supermodels?

I was in the arms of the Rock God. Rock royalty. While Terri had Billy Ocean dancing at her feet, we had a record rep hustling us to a waiting limo.

I said, "But this is Robert Plant."

She goes, "I know. I get it. I do, but I will literally get fired if you're not on this flight. You're nominated tonight, and the plane is waiting." Then she said something odd. "Why don't you ask him to come back to London with you?"

Wow! That stopped me dead in my tracks. I was like, could I do that? Could I cross over that line? Hell, yes! Why can't I do that? I *could* ask him to come with me!

So, I did. I asked him, I mean, his hands felt so damn good on me, his low voice lovely to my ear. "Robert, would you come back to London with me tonight for this award show thingy I have to attend? Just for a little bit, please...I really have to go to this thing, but I really want to stay with you," I plead to Robert Plant.

He was quiet for a few moments, I thought seriously contemplating my offer. He then looked at me straight into my eyes and said, "Darlin', I don't do award shows."

I now looked at him and I'm thinking, *who says that?* But I mean, he says that of course. He says that! He's Robert Fucking Plant!

A memorable night spent hunkered down in a hotel room having drinks, listening to his stories and other things never happened. What did happen was a kiss that was captured on film. A kiss he landed on my cheek before I headed out to sing, boarding the plane to London later that evening without him.

Back in the US with a management team finally in place, I'd no longer have to travel without a manager. The ever-important buffer between me, the record companies, and the constant daily demands, my manager also became my confidante and liaison between me and any choice and decision and desire I had. We headed back to London to tape *Top of the Pops* TV show with my Glam Squad in tow.

There was a young technician nervously trying to hook a microphone to my bustier.

"Here, let me help you with that," I said. He was tall with beautiful hair, very handsome, and very young. After the interview, I climbed into the limo with my crew to go to the hotel. I turned to my manager, "Hey, go ask that kid for his number and ask him to come meet us at the hotel, too."

"What the hell? I'm not doing that. I'm not a pimp." Then he realized he left something in the studio. "Damn, I forgot my hat."

"See, that's God telling you to get in there and get this done," I said with a smile. I had my makeup artist, Sergeant Carter, and my stylist, Cloud Cummings, as we laughed and giggled. My glam squad. They knew what I was up to.

He probably traumatized that kid, who did end up coming to the Mayfair Hotel that night. He was a great guy and traveled with me all over the world. He was 19. I called him Manchild.

We usually stayed at the Mayfair although the European paparazzi had become increasingly aggressive as my popularity grew. They would follow us on motorcycles with cameras trained on me, trying to get that elusive photo. Now here I was with a 19-year-old and my crew giggling around me.

While I was handling the demands overseas, Ric was at the studio in Glen Cove compiling music and songs for the album that we needed. He would play music over the phone for me so that when I got back, we could get started on the album that the record company was demanding. With the success of "Tell It to My Heart," we now had writers asking to work with us. I had previously done a demo on a song called "Don't Rush Me," which I thought could work. Arista had input as well. Clive Davis, the president, insisted that one of the songs had to be "I'll Always Love You." I hadn't dealt with him personally yet, it was more of an Oz situation since I was just signed for the single at first. I wasn't happy with the song choice because I didn't understand how to make the song work.

Ric assured me that it would be ok. "Let's just do it because Arista really wants it. Clive is the one you wanted to work with. We will make it work."

When I got back to the States, I immediately went into the studio with Ric. There was no time to waste. With our plan in place, we got down to business. I was happy to be in one place and not have to travel for a while. The biggest issue was that I was still living in an apartment in Long Beach on the boardwalk facing the ocean. Fame came swiftly, and pretty soon there went my anonymity and privacy as fans congregated on the boardwalk yelling up to my townhouse. I had gotten my wish. I was famous and recognized and people knew who I was. And now I needed to move.

I would sneak out my back door, jump into my car, and hole up in the studio with my crew: Ric, Bobby, Ritchie, and the others. That was my safe haven, and by then we were a well-oiled machine. Yet now there was tremendous pressure from the record company, something we hadn't dealt with before. It put a strain on both of us to live up to the two singles, do good work, and do it fast. Not only that, I was still responsible for doing promotion as it was never ending and always needed. It was a tough balancing act physically, emotionally, and mentally. I carry my instrument within my body. I don't have the luxury to pack it away in a case for the night when the show is done. Over time, vocal strain and lack of sleep left me at my ENT office and taking a steroid as my voice was under constant strain.

Having Champion Entertainment in place as my management, more control and order were developed and so was my health and welfare. My voice was still under enormous strain and challenged physically due to travel, interviews, shows, recordings, and daily press.

That first album ended up with ten songs: "Tell It to My

Heart," "In the Darkness," "Don't Rush Me," "I'll Always Love You," "Prove Your Love" (same writers of "Tell It to My Heart"), "Do You Want It Right Now," "Carry Your Heart," "Want Ads," "Where Does That Boy Hang Out," and "Upon the Journey's End" (a duet with Billy T. Scott).

Our happy team of musical geniuses pulled through. Ric Wake, my musical soul mate, Bob Cadway the mixing and engineer guru of all my vocals who also played a mean Les Paul guitar, Richie Cannata on saxophone, Ritchie Jones, and Rich Tancredi. It was amazing that we created such a solid album in eight weeks.

The first single, "Tell It to My Heart," charted on the *Billboard Hot 100* in October of 1987 and weeks later it was in the *Top 40*. In January of 1988, "Tell It to My Heart" hit the *Top Ten* and stayed there for 25 weeks. It reached number four on the US Dance charts. In the UK, the song went all the way to number three in 1988 and was the 23rd best-selling single of that year. The song was in the top five in Belgium, Ireland, Norway, Spain, and Sweden and went to number one in Austria, Germany, The Netherlands, and Switzerland. In 1988, it was certified gold in Germany, Sweden, and the US.

The label released "Prove Your Love" in April of 1988 as the second single and it climbed to number seven on the *Billboard Hot 100* and stayed in the Top 40 for eleven weeks and number one on the Dance charts. It went to number four in Germany and eight in the UK. It was a number one hit in Switzerland.

The third single was Clive's first real imprint on the album, a song he felt I needed to record, "I'll Always Love You." It was released in September of 1988. Although I was not a fan of the song initially, there was no denying the impact it had on my credibility as a female vocalist to contend with and as an artist crossing over into the R&B and Adult Contemporary charts. Clive proved me wrong. It was a huge hit. Not only had I dominated pop, dance, and adult contemporary, I was now in the R&B charts. On the *Billboard Hot 100* it reached number three. On the Adult Contemporary it was number two, and it also charted in the UK, Switzerland, Germany, France, Australia, and Italy. The video was shot stylistically in black and white, my ex-boyfriend playing my love interest. My hair bigger than ever, like Dolly Parton big.

When Arista released my fourth single, "Don't Rush Me," it

hit number two on the Hot 100, number three on Adult Contemporary, and number six on the Dance chart. With my interest in fashion and the photographers of the day dominating videos, my image was being controlled because it was more important than ever. Alex Keshishian, known later for Madonna's *Truth or Dare* documentary, was the deputy director at the helm of the camera.

Even though the first single was released in 1987, it wasn't until 1988 that the album was released and I was Grammy-nominated for Best Female R&B Vocal for "I'll Always Love You" and Best R&B Song. I was nominated for Best Pop Vocal Performance, Female, for the *Tell It to My Heart* album, and Record of the Year. The album was also nominated for multiple New York Music Awards, with me winning Best Dance Artist. In 1989, I was nominated for an American Music Award in the Favorite Pop/Rock New Artist category. The album continued to sweep the awards.

♭

FAME, LIKE THE SONG, is intoxicating. Powerful. Senses go wild for fame. Yet, how toxic it can become. My experience was no different from most who have experienced it. I don't have many regrets about it, but I have a few. With the chaotic blur of constant movement, my requirements to stay prolific and keep ever charting to maintain a high profile, toxicity wasn't far behind. One's clarity can become so dull because there's no time to go within. The externals are dominating your day to day. It's very difficult to take a breath. And that's the way I can rationalize some of my decision-making at the time.

I was doing my part to stay high-profile. *People* magazine did an article on me with the title "Taylor Dayne, a Tough Cookie with an Album, Heart, of Gold." They pointed out how I was a Jewish girl from Long Island who made it still living modestly in an apartment with a Pontiac Grand Am.

Rule #1: Being famous and being rich are TWO VERY different things. I learned that then. The illusion and image we see is not what's real necessarily. At the time, I was only making money through advances given to me to live on by the record company. I was now responsible for other people who were depending on me for their salaries and livelihood. The pressures were mounting and responsibilities becoming very real.

The fame that I enjoyed overseas was now a reality on the home front. Things were moving at a breakneck pace. Having a strong work ethic will always be part of my success, and also my fear of failure and losing control. Paying one's dues is really boot camp and it's paramount to success. For me all those long nights sitting on different stages, working at the Russian club singing six to seven hours a night, built my strength and foundation. I don't quit.

The energy it takes to sustain momentum when you're in the wave of success is mind-blowing, and as I was no different than most, the wave crashed at times and constantly pulled in many directions. Ric and I were still equal partners in Bleux Productions, but I couldn't help feeling that most of the load was resting on my shoulders. While he was back at the studio in one place, I was out there in the front lines, and it started to eat away at me.

I was a full-on pop star. It was an amazing feeling to walk into any room and be instantly recognized, validated, and admired. It's intoxicating, yet you must back that up. At the end of the day, I was just a little girl with my anxieties hidden inside. I couldn't run from my issues. I had just put them on hold. Maybe I put them on hold knowing I had the strength, stamina, and energy to do the work. I knew there was a plan for me. I was using my gift and people now were responding. My preparation met the opportunity and my "overnight success" was the glorious result. Dreaming of a moment is not the same as living in a moment. I don't think anyone is truly prepared for that kind of success. The reality is never quite what you think it will be, and I was fine with that. I was accustomed to hard work. I felt more alive than ever. Joyful, scared, living in the moment more than I ever could in the past. Irrational fears loomed in my life now. I was living breathless moments at breakneck speeds. Some of my greatest, often scared-shitless-a-lot-of-the-time moments turned into some of my greatest life lessons. Just some of my greatest hits.

As my third single, "I'll Always Love You," was released, I headed back to Germany and the UK for more promotion. I was scheduled to perform on a TV show in Berlin and then accept the Berolina Award for Best Female Artist of the Year. This was an honor Tina Turner had won the year before. This was huge. I was now an artist to be reckoned with as my fourth single was charting around the world.

In Hamburg on a rare night off, Terri, my record rep, and I wanted to go see Prince on the *LoveSexy* tour. We were ushered into the VIP section of the arena to watch Prince in all his phenomenal glory. In the first half hour, a large guard with an earpiece (who turned out to be Prince's brother) walked up to Terri and whispered, "Is this Taylor Dayne?"

Terri always spoke for me and people knew to go to her. "Yes."

He said, "Prince would like to extend an invite for Taylor to join him at his after show."

I leaned over and said, "Yes, we will be there."

Terri echoed, "Yes, she will be there." Lol!

The greatness of Prince the artist, his musicianship, his incredible live stage persona performances, his overt sexuality. After a full concert, it was not unusual for him and company to take over a smaller venue, an after-hours club, and entertain for an intimate audience for another two to three hours. Endless energy poured out of him in the late hours as his band joined him onstage.

Just coming off the *Bad Tour*, I was back in Germany doing some promo TV shows in Hamburg. I spent so much time in Germany between '87-'89 that I dated a rock star named Bela from the band Die Arzte. We had met at an awards show. He was the Slash of the German version of Guns N' Roses and the face of the band. The two of us together generated a lot of pandemonium and media frenzy as we cruised around Berlin on his Harley when he would drop me at my hotel or interviews as cars and scooters would chase us around the cities. It was surreal, fun, sometimes scary, and very rock star.

Bela flew to Hamburg and joined me to see Prince at the club. At one point, I said I need to pee, so naturally all the girls make for the restroom. As we walked down the stairs of the balcony, I saw an ascending staircase to the left of the restroom door. I saw a heel, then a white pair of pants with letters "E" then an "X" then a "Y" then an "S" as it came closer. I was trying to put the letters together in my mind and read "LOVESEXY." And there in front of us was none other than The One and Only Prince.

The three of us stood there speechless. Prince stared eye-level with me in his tight, one-piece bodysuit and just stared and chewed gum noisily. Eventually someone finally spoke. It was him.

As he looked at me, he said, "What's your name?"

I said, "Taylor."

He squinted his eyes. "Taylor what?" Still chewing.

"Dayne."

He chewed for a second and then broke out into a wide grin. He slapped his leg and said, "Girl, I've been wanting to meet you for a long time."

Fireworks would best describe the moments after that. I looked at Terri, and she was basically butter on the floor. I didn't care that he only came up to my chin. This was Prince and he was fine as hell! Smacking his gum. Smiling at me. Telling jokes. Laughing. Full of life. His bodyguard brother standing beside him and watching the whole interaction.

Then he said, "Girl, I saw you last week in Montreux. You killed it! You can sing."

We stood there, us girls, with shit-eating grins across our faces. Not knowing what to say, I was watching and studying him. My head was buzzing. I had just seen him in concert take over a stadium and now we're outside a bathroom in some Red Light District club and he was talking to me. Prince was funny. And bubbly. And he was chewing that gum like nobody's goddamn business. But when he stuck it out of his mouth, almost like a snake tongue or something, then it was my turn to say damn, WTF?

I couldn't control myself. Instinctively, I put my hand out to grab whatever was falling out of his mouth.

He jumped back saying, "Girl, what are you doing reaching into my mouth?"

"I don't know. I thought you were dropping your gum. What were you doing with it?" We all burst out laughing at the same time. I thought he was trying to spit it out and my Jewish mother instinct took over.

Then he stopped laughing and looked at me seriously and said, "I want you to come on stage and sing with me."

I said "What?" like I didn't hear him.

"I want you to come on stage and sing with me."

"Are you serious?"

"Girl, yes, I'm serious. You're going to come up and sing with me."

I was petrified. I looked at Terri. "Can she come with me?"

"What?" He looked over at the beautiful Terri up and down and turned to his bodyguard, "No problem. Bring her up, too."

Then he turned to me and smiled. "See you in a bit."

As he headed to the back of the stage, his brother added, "We'll come get you."

We stood there as Prince walked off backstage. We beelined into the bathrooms as we began girl-screaming in unison for a complete five minutes! I'm not kidding. We didn't know what to do with all that energy, all that love, all that fame, all that SEX, all that everything! Where does all that energy go? It was fandemonium. We were the fans now. This was Prince. This was next-level shit. I was "new fame," but he was established. *He was fame.*

When we finally, I mean *finally*, caught our breath and found our shit, we got back upstairs as the entire club stared at us. Bela just looked at us like three crazy girls who had just left the prom when Prince hit the stage with his Purple Rain, LoveSexy, and Controversy gear including his purple guitar, a white baby grand, and several wind machines. At some point, Prince landed himself at the piano and in a gospel-esque style sang, "I need some help up here! Can I get some help up here? Can I get some Taylor help up here?"

My heart jumped as I realized he was saying my name and I looked at Terri in a panic. The same bodyguard was looming in front of us, and in a Lurch-like voice said, "You ready?"

I was thinking, *No, oh my God, no, I can't do this!* Oh, dear God! It was the same feeling I'd had opening for Michael, running up that ramp, jumping off the gangplank, and being pushed into the arms of the audience.

As the bodyguard took my hand, I grabbed Terri as hard as I could, dragging her with me. We walked around behind the stage, the crowd parting for us. I saw Prince at the piano talking to his audience. He sang, "I want some help up here." Then he looked over at me and nodded his head for me to come forward.

I said, "What does he want?"

The bodyguard said, "Go up to him."

I was scared shitless. *No way!* Prince kept nodding toward me, so I finally crept over there and kneeled by the piano.

He said, "Take my mic."

"What?"

He said, "Go take my mic."

"Which mic?"

"The one in the middle of the stage, girl!"

As Sheila E. was banging on the drums and smiling at me, I asked, "Can Terri come with me?"

"What? You crazy, girl."

"Well, can I take her?"

"Yes, take the girl. Go!"

I was taking her anyway. Didn't matter what he said. She was my secret weapon. We slowly walked over to the mic at the front of the stage, all eyes on us.

Still at his piano, Prince sang, "We got some Taylor Dayne in here! I got some help in here!" Everyone went nuts.

As the wind machines lifted every extension on my head, I added, "And a little Terri Rojers!" Moments I'll never forget.

He asked me to sing along to a song I'd never heard before. I looked at Terri and she smiled her never-ending smile, just like she did in the Russian club. If she didn't know the lyrics, it didn't matter. She smiled and pinched me as we stumbled through the gospel song he was making up on the spot. As he stopped the song once to correct my lyrics, I smiled just like Terri had taught me and kept singing just like Terri taught me. I sang the wrong words. He corrected me. Nothing mattered. There was electricity in that room that you can't define.

Two weeks later the electricity continued when Prince asked me to join him in Minneapolis at Paisley Park with Chaka Kahn, Sheila E. and several other artists. More moments I'll always love and treasure. Always.

♭

THIRTY YEARS LATER, I wonder, is fame fleeting, is it continuous? Now is an extraordinary time for me. I'm celebratory and ever-grateful as I can see the link after link building chain after chain in this incredible connection from my soul to people around me, to fans, and others I've never even met. An artist shares with an audience. It's their ability to share, their ability to speak in a language called music, "the arts." We call it that because we don't have a better word for it, but fame is magic. Yet, it can be fleeting and devastating even as the accolades are coming and records are being broken.

Many years later, after evaluating my career, having self-reflection, it is true that artists are their harshest critic. Coming off that first tour, it was almost two years of constant promotion ultimately leading into performances throughout Europe and the United States, my life was changed forever. The good, the bad, and the ugly. The difficulties of taking moments for myself to catch my breath. The tug-of-war between "Leslie" and the fame of "Taylor." The suppression of the girl I used to be emerging into the woman I wanted to be, from losing hair extensions and baby fat to walking into womanhood. The struggle between my record label, my manager, and now my soul.

Returning to a home after two years, it felt like what coming home from a war must be like. The people aren't the same. You're not treated the same. Yet part of you just wanted to go home and be nurtured and be loved and feel safe. Home was now a new place I needed to create for myself. I felt broken and tired.

As the months went by, pressures didn't subside after the tour and the release of my first record. I had a new record to make and a sophomore slump to break. Renegotiating my record deal was paramount for my new management. It should have happened when my first single dropped and became a sensation, but we waited an album later. Now I had five Top Ten singles and I was a certified multi-platinum-selling artist around the world. The deal was still the one we'd negotiated with the record promotor, and my management was anxious to renegotiate my contract with the label. So was I, because I needed money to live.

With a new contract in place, I got a million dollars which was actually the residuals owed from the first album. The first thing I did was to buy a house. I needed a home where I felt safe and secure. Basically, this was a loan. It wasn't my money, although it should have been. They were just handing me the money I'd earned for them with the first record. It was a financial shell game, moving the money around, hiding it.

The blurred lines between business managers, attorneys, and management meant conflicts of interest were quite common. CEOs and record label presidents were represented by the same people representing me. Deals were rarely in the interest of the artist with 5% to the business manager, 10% the agency, 20% to management. With all the expenses and recoupment fees, what is an artist left with? The system is set up for only one winner unless you go back in and start fighting. It's like getting a bad bank loan. When the bottom falls out of the market, the lenders and the lawyers get paid first, and you're stuck with the payments.

With that money I moved off the Long Beach boardwalk and made an adult decision to buy a home. My first home. It couldn't be just any home. I was on the south shore and needed to move to the north shore. That's where Ric suggested I go. Long Island was divided by the Robert Moses Causeway, the Seaford-Oyster Bay Expressway and the Long Island Expressway. Those highways might as well have been paved with millions of dollars because the north shore was appropriately called The Gold Coast. That's where the "old money" retreated back in the day. Then it was "new money" with Ric Wake, Dee Snider, Billy Joel, Debbie Gibson, and me. I wanted to find my perfect home and make a statement. That was the next step for me.

I fell in love with the inherent beauty of the north shore of Long Island. Walking along the Long Island Sound every day, going into the woods, looking at the opulent mansions perched on graceful hills. It was the home of aristocracy, where the Tiffanys, Vanderbilts, and Roosevelts went to escape the madness of New York. This is where I was going now to escape the madness of my career.

I fell in love with a beautiful historic Victorian that was built in 1850 with 8,500 square feet, a three-acre lawn, barn, tennis court, pool, and a history of ghosts for days. It was a secluded retreat in an exclusive community where I felt safe. There was private law enforcement just down the hill. I felt like this could be home. This was where I wanted to be.

During this break while putting my body back together, my love of reading continued. My collection of books started to grow. I no longer had to rely on the thousand-page works of Larry McMurtry and James Michener to get through a tour. Some found those books intimidating, but to me they were friends. They allowed me to escape the chaos and live in another time and another place. I'd now keep books stacked beside my bed, no longer having to pack them in suitcases. Reading was my drug of choice.

I also continued to focus on health and wellness to put myself back together piece by piece. As I went deeper inside, I needed to clean up what I felt had gotten so dirty. I turned to books by Louise Hay, Marianne Williamson, and Julia Cameron's *The Artist's Way*. They gave me better tools to live by and helped me regain my confidence away from a hotel room, tour bus, or plane. In my new home, I promised myself a slow but sure healing and those books were my bibles.

Og Mandino's *The Greatest Miracle* got me through my initial panic attacks, so I sent Og a letter to tell him how much his work has inspired me. He sent back the most beautiful letter. We spoke a couple of times on the phone and a lovely relationship grew. I even thanked him on my first record and created Greatest Miracle Publishing Company and Corporation to honor his beautiful words and a hope flame that will be forever held in my heart. My belief systems were building and growing. I was becoming stronger again and able to take care of myself with the impactful words, messages, affirmations, and mantras from those authors.

With Ric now living up the road, the studio was within a ten-minute drive. Clive had been like the wizard behind the curtain, like Charlie on the speakerphone directing the angels, for the first album. The next one was a different story. Everyone was on board, everyone was involved, and the sophomore record was important. Clive was now at the helm and he wouldn't let me forget it.

It was an easier process on one level because thought was put into it and I was grateful that we were a team now working together, not playing catch up. We had built a team of songs and sounds. Ric knew he had to outdo himself after the first record. I needed to make sure the songs represented me as I was now as a successful artist. Top songwriters were coming to the table like Diane Warren. In his office, Clive played some of her songs for me. Then he said, "I was holding this song for Whitney, but I feel it's better suited for you." When I heard "Love Will Lead You Back," I knew it was a beautiful, incredible ballad. He had proved me wrong with "I'll Always Love You," so I knew better than to test Clive when it came to ballads. His instincts were so finely tuned.

Ric and I worked well together compiling music for the new record, even though my management had forced us to dissolve Bleux Productions. It was a tough choice to make and I know it hurt Ric. But at the end of the day, they made more money and I made more money. Ric was now a top producer in demand being pulled in different directions that did not involve me. I was jealous and hurt that he would work with other female artists. Those were difficult waters to navigate. Ric and I always had a common goal. The music. We were on the same page. Now Clive was pulling the strings. He wanted to make sure the next record was a hit and so did we.

After I'd toured the world and played huge stadiums, I was asked to do a showcase in New York City for a VIP audience of press and industry insiders at The Bitter End for an audience of 400 people. Clive wanted to introduce me as his newest hit artist. After playing venues of 40,000, coming to a small club was shocking. I didn't realize that I needed to match my energy with the size of the venue.

A review came out after the show that said I was "ferocious like a lion" and that I "tore up the room." I realized that I needed to match my energy to the crowd. Another experience and another lesson learned. Now that I was in the public eye, I was also getting critiqued and criticized as well as applauded. I hadn't learned not to read reviews and I took some things to heart. I had to accept thoughts and comments on my hair, my face, my looks, my boobs, my body, my clothes, my style, and now my voice and my tone. Welcome to fame and fortune. Welcome to celebrity.

I was now a cog in the corporate machine. Being a woman in the music industry in 1989, I was expected to perform night after night and look good doing it. I understood that. Looking good was powerful. Looking good was a powerful tool. I wanted to deliver that. I wanted to deliver power, confidence, independence. I felt that. I wanted to emulate that beauty, that glamor, that style that I'd admired in those magazines. I was a young woman delving into something I knew nothing about, yet I was passionate about it, which meant I could never be wrong. Feelings are never wrong.

Improving myself was paramount because I wouldn't have the energy if I didn't. Working toward a higher greatness, a bigger truth, a greater purpose was now my truth and my mantra. What is my purpose? For my second record, what is my real voice? I took it to heart. Who couldn't? That's the trappings of fame. You're open prey. Whether I knew it or not, strength, stamina, staying real, being in control, being treated fairly, being a woman with a voice was becoming an important part of my story. Struggling to keep my integrity in my looks, my style, and my music, I was determined to not let the business shake me down and get everything out of me. I held on tight to that belief, my hope flame that everything would work out. The loss would be where I was before and that was not an option, losing control.

The one place where I felt safe was in the studio. When Ric and I were together, the noise was drowned out. We were locked in a beautiful cell making music and speaking the same language. I was back with my team. It was like a warm blanket, and I stayed wrapped in it. With the album coming together and Ric and I co-writing several songs, our hearts were filled up in that studio.

When the album *Can't Fight Fate* was done, the final tracks were: "With Every Beat of My Heart," "I'll Be Your Shelter," "Love Will Lead You Back," "Heart of Stone," "You Can't Fight Fate," "Up all Night," "I Know the Feeling," "Wait for Me," and Ric and I snuck on two of our co-writes, "You Meant the World to Me" and "Ain't No Good."

I was grateful for the album and followed most of Clive's "advice." My sophomore record was a success, eventually certified double-platinum. I had a lot of respect for Clive and Arista and what we had accomplished. He would often talk to me in his office saying, "You're like a daughter to me. You remind me of a young Janis Joplin, of a young Tina Turner." I did feel like a daughter to him on some level, and I felt a connection to him. He provided fatherly guidance for me, but when things didn't go his way it could quickly turn harsh and unaccepting.

Unlike a father where love should be unconditional, this was not. This was the music business and I took things personally. I needed to remember this was a business. If we didn't share the same vision, my opinion was not as important as his. My thoughts were not as important as his. He had history and experience behind him. And years of wisdom and success I did not. As a woman, I felt small. As a "daughter," I felt smaller. What was best for him and the company was not always what was best for me. Mostly, I felt invalidated and unheard.

"You look like a whore in this video."

"You look cheap and slutty."

"Watch Lisa Stansfield."

"Look at Whitney."

"Listen to this song."

The blurry line of my childhood, of fatherly guidance and care which could quickly turn harsh when things didn't go as planned. Like any child, there comes a time when self-assertion and independence is needed for growth and separation.

My past was once again living in the present as it was so deeply rooted into the rocky foundation of my childhood soul.

How can I sing what he wants me to sing?

How can I wear what he wants me to wear?

How can I be what he wants me to be?

The little voice inside was very sad.

# CHAPTER 5
## Woman Who Runs with Wolves

BEING DIRECT. Being blunt. Being honest. The same character traits that save you, can sink you, too. "Be careful what you wish for, you just might get it." Yes indeed.

After years of climbing the mountain of fame, success brought a lot of "yes" people into my life. I maintained a good enough BS meter coming from NY. In my personal relationships, I could generally weed out the users. But in business I found the blurred lines far more difficult to navigate, to separate the two while I lived within the very walls of my career.

"It's not personal, it's business." It was hard to discern between the two when every record and every song felt like a pregnancy and a birth. I was personally invested in the process and in creating a lasting message, so when I started getting haters and naysayers, I couldn't help but take it personally and feel wounded. Cause I did. I ams who I ams (Popeye). Honest to a fault.

Taking charge, my ingrained, fear-ridden survival mechanism to control my environment, control the chaos, came back and fit like an old glove. In my teens, I became my own mental health drill sergeant. Taking charge of my sanity was crucial to my survival. As my body lived in fear stored in my guts, "live through this" was a competition I had with myself. Like in the hospital years ago. Get through it. Head down, grit your teeth, and run like hell out of the woods.

Walking away from what I worked so hard to run to was a frightening time for me as well as a relief. It was always easier for me to go out and get what I wanted and fight my own battles if I understood them.

I was often associated with the tough New York girl stereotype, yet my emotional intelligence and healing said the opposite. I'd learned to be careful of my thoughts because they became my actions. *Be careful of your actions because they become your habits. Be careful of your habits because they become your character.*

Being a determined woman, being able to handle what was thrown at me was a survival mechanism. Nothing short of it. Soon, whatever personal relationships I could possibly have while traveling the world began to run the same course.

Leaving Leslie behind? I wanted to distance myself from old me. Easy.

Leaving the Russian club and walking into the arms of fame? Passion, work.

Maintaining a loving relationship? Hard.

Two people with two different perspectives and values trying to lovingly become this "entity," this relationship, while maintaining one's own identity? Impossible.

In my 20s and early 30s, it was all about my needs. They seemed most important at the time because everyone needed a piece of me. The people I was with during those times reflected those needs. It gave me strength to surround myself with people in "the industry" who could understand my daily needs and juggle what I was going through.

Moving from one relationship to the next, whether it was in a few months or a couple of years, people's lives were affected. Hearts were affected. I left an effect on others. Being on tour for months at a time, the bus is your house, your family, your crew. Relationships? Well, they happened on the road, or with whoever could handle me being on the road and drop what they were doing to meet me in somewhereville. Those were the ones I had relationships with. As my career continued to soar and move in an ever-demanding direction, relationships would fall by the wayside. Sadly, some of those relationships ended in hotel rooms, on phone calls, or fax. I was on a different path. Moving in a different direction. I wasn't able to face disappointment in relationships. I couldn't face disappointing men, nor could I face a standoff.

I know I hurt some hearts. My Russian boyfriend who fell in love with the confident punky-shmunky girl whose voice mesmerized him. It was bad timing as I was leaving the club, breaking out, and taking off as an artist.

It saddened me that I couldn't continue, and I did feel guilty because I hurt some good men—the Austrian, the Russian, the German. They did love, I just was not prepared for it. I more often just needed closeness and grounding. Hurting another is never fun. My sensitivity to their feelings was strong, and I felt guilt when I disappointed them. But I felt propelled forward and couldn't stop the train, my tour manager often left with the task of delivering the fatal news. As I got more famous, I didn't walk away feeling very proud of myself.

Feeling worthy was now something I had to live with, worthy enough for what was happening to me. Receiving fame, success, and wealth so suddenly (my destiny, my dream), I didn't have the tools and skills to deal with it. How can you accept wealth, abundance, and love when you're not in love with yourself? Truth.

So, I did what most do when wealth is the "king thing" that proves someone's value. I bought a mansion. It was proof of my worth. Literally. It was physical proof I could afford to be happy, right? Wrong. More than anything, I was mentally, physically, and emotionally empty, exhausted after almost two years of constant motion. What I wanted was to show off. What I needed was a safe place. A sacred place. A home of my own. I knew I had to start somewhere, piecing myself back together. That home, the mansion, marked the first time I built something safe for me and it was an act of self-love. During the five years we lived in that home, I had some of my biggest breakthroughs, and core relationships and friendships and family I still cherish. My home was built around my needs, but it became a home for many who needed the same things.

My house manager, or roommate (you choose), was an older girlfriend I met twenty years prior to my fame. She knew me well and was like a big sister to me—Lisa or "Gallotta" as everyone calls her. Professionally, she worked and managed VIP investments at a bank, so I figured she could manage my house, all ten bedrooms and three acres and grounds with a horse and a barn and a pool. So, I asked Lisa to move in.

Did I mention she was from Brooklyn? LOL. Her in the woods was a sight. I was traveling extensively to pay now for "the White

Elephant," barely there at times, but bills need to be paid and a house needs to be maintained. Semi-adulthood. I was 25 years old to her 32.

As Lisa took over the third floor of the historic Victorian mansion, soon we made it a home, a safe place where our circle of friendships bloomed, and new friendships blossomed. As young women, we had each other's back and it didn't hurt that I had money to pay the bills.

Soon, my home became a sort of retreat for all, with enough bedrooms and space for everyone to take refuge and serve one another. Our long weekends were Friday afternoons to Monday mornings when most would leave, some in car, some on the LIRR, back to the city or Brooklyn. Her circle of friends became mine, and mine hers, still to this day. The cooking that went on in this house was often next level with Gallota behind the pots and pans, and Debra, her winger, or Leeanne taking over with every fresh herb and vegetable conceivable. We all would eat and cook and drink and cry and laugh and laugh and drink. And it was the talks, the sharing and the walks we all took, as I lived in a private community with beautiful hiking trails along the beach and the woods.

These women became a foundational anchor in my life. I provided the space, and they created a unique retreat and lifestyle of friendships and wounded birds. Some family members were biological as my brothers, Lisa's mom Martha, and her bestie Tim were always there cooking and laughing and loving life. Others always welcome.

During this time, I had an awakening of sisterhood, of our power in numbers, and of how so many girls could get along. I provided the shelter and the beautiful sanctuary, Lisa the soul of the house, who cooked following my nonfat guidelines. LeeAnne, Debra, Diana, Kelly, Nancy, Paulette, Todd, and Martha provided the food and wine and love for all who needed a safe place to lay their heads. For five years we lived in this suspended reality of parties and concerts, boys, and girls, touring and money, living the dream as some would say.

My need to feel safe, always a dominate energy within me, continued to lead me to men who on the outside looked strong and capable in their physical strength, their mental strength.

These were attractive qualities to me in a man. He could take charge, take control, handle anything.

My real life was still geographically challenging. I was constantly traveling, but now being in a relationship to me felt grounding and important. I went from a Brooklyn teamster to a Greek actor from Queens who had a day job. "I'm the egg man, just making deliveries, Taylor." Life was fun and committal in a non-committal way. I was always in something, mostly a series of monogamous relationships that lasted less than a year, floating from one to the next.

The demands from the record label to finish my third studio album were high. Clive and I were clashing on songs and material, me wanting to spread my creative wings, feeling that after selling millions of records and having eight top-ten hits I reserved the right to voice my thoughts and opinions, and be creatively involved as I was in the beginning of my career.

The music business was in NYC. Soon I was in the city three to four days a week working, recording, writing, partying, and loving life. NYC in 1992 was on fire. My best friends were the "It" in music, fashion, PR, design, and events—promoters, photographers, chefs, artists. Kelly and Ronnie Cutrone, Jason Weinberg, Patrick McMullan, Debbie Harry, Dianne Brill, Michael Schmidt, Downtown Julie Brown—it was an exciting time in NY.

We were breaking out and breaking the rules. Being in *Page Six* once a week was a common result, restaurants our social meeting spots. Food and clubs evolving within hotels becoming lifestyle brands with art and music and fashion connecting the dots.

I MET "THE CHEF" at a dinner Kelly Cutrone and Michael Schmidt threw. Debbie Harry was there, Ronnie Cutrone, Diane Brille, Anita Sarko, all friends, all in that scene. I can't say I really remember much as I was doing the usual "three dirty martinis." But I will always remember meeting The Chef that night at the dinner. He was shy and aloof and seemed a bit pretentious to me. So, I went back to my martinis, but later as we went clubbing and he tagged along, not drinking, (I thought very odd) but laughing at everything I said (flattering but odd), he seemed very intense and yet attentive to me. His stare was hot, and he smelled yummy (Chanel

Egoiste) as he got nearer to me to be heard over the loud music. He was different, not quite as masculine as I normally went for. He was an artist, a chef. He was divorced, and 36 to my 27 years old, on the "Hot List" in *Interview* magazine as a top emerging chef to watch. He was handsome.

I was crashing at Kelly's apartment which was typical when I was in the city. The Chef and I were in the same cab. When we pulled up to her building, he looked at me and asked for my number. I had not expected that after a long-ass night of drinking and partying.

I looked at him and said, "A date? You want to go on a date with me?"

He giggled almost and said, "Yes, can I take you to dinner?"

I was a bit surprised.

"Okay? I guess. Sure."

Up in the apartment, Kelly said, "The Chef likes you." I was like huh? I was just so not thinking or feeling much of anything. It got me to thinking. He got me to stop. To feel. And I wasn't doing much of that.

I still smile thinking of our first date because it was really my first date ever. Honestly, up until that time in my life, I fell into relationships; literally I woke up and I was in one. No discussion just "yup, we're together." I actually liked that quality about myself. *Don't take things too seriously until they do something serious.* So, this was really a first-time experience for me. I just didn't know it at the time.

As I was home in Long Island getting ready, I decided to drive into the city. I also knew I was gonna be late. I was a diva for sure and being late was natural. I guess he didn't get the memo. No cell phones then either. Even crazier, he actually lived at The Plaza Hotel as that's where he worked, brought in by Ivanka herself. I knew as I headed out that I was already forty-minutes late for our date, so I could either pull over and find a payphone or keep driving and get to the city.

I finally pulled up to The Plaza, and he was nowhere downstairs. I rang his room. When he came downstairs, he looked so lovely and sad, his first words were, "I thought you weren't coming."

I felt it. Right there. The first time in a long time. His sadness was so sincere. My heart just opened, and I realized my actions had consequences. I said, "I'm so sorry. I was never *not* coming. I was just in a lot of traffic, and I was just running late."

He said, "But I cancelled our reservation." Wow, he had made a reservation. Then he said, "I can call them and see if they'll take us now." Yes, please.

When we finally did get to the restaurant, it was so romantic. I remember the feeling. At this point he had my full attention and we were not on guard. I had already hurt him. When he ordered for me, I felt cared for. When he held the door for me, I felt all the little, lovely, integral things that make one feel wanted and admired. He warmed me up in the right ways. I wasn't used to it. I was now officially out of my comfort zone, not being in control, and I really liked it.

Here I was, not on stage but in a restaurant, with a man who was admiring me. At that moment, I looked at him and that's when I felt those incredible butterflies in my stomach. A feeling of desire and warmth washed over me. This was different. His mind was different. As we continued our night, he picked the wine and ordered things I might enjoy as he asked me what I liked. He was curious. He was a reader like me. He was in therapy. He was sincere and serious, and a star in his own profession, in his own right. So, when he kissed me at the end of the night it was everything. I swooned. I knew I would follow this man.

I'd never felt this deep and soulful a connection or need for somebody as I did for The Chef. As we became an "it" couple, there was an excitement to dating somebody with his own notoriety and his own success. I felt a mixture of desire and pride for him, and I felt loved and beautiful when the light shown on us. It's when the light fades into darkness that the trouble begins.

It was difficult having a relationship, trying to relate with somebody while you're both managing successful, explosive careers, the two of us wounded on different levels in different ways in childhood, coming together to heal. He was working through his divorce in therapy, and me working on my fear of losing control. When disagreements arose, my old patterns kicked in, and so did his. Mine was to run off like my father or blow up and leave. His was to shut down, sometimes for weeks, overwhelmed emotionally he'd say, out of the blue, "I can't do this anymore."

The first time this happened, I was devastated. It took him two weeks before he called me in sadness and remorse saying he wanted to get back together and was "sorry for the silence." I was elated to be back with him, but now a little nervous. When a month later, he did the same thing, I was devastated. Things were good, and he "just couldn't do it" again? I was at a loss. We were now in an unhealthy pattern of breakups and makeups. I was out of control and suggested since he was in therapy that we try couple's counseling. To me it seemed the only way we could continue, inside I knew that.

Years of mental anguish for me had led to extensive counseling I'd done on myself between the ages of 15 to 20. So, these last seven years were my first years of complete freedom. I was able to travel alone, without a panic attack, without the disabling fear that I thought I would die from it.

This freedom was intoxicating for me, but so was his love. Even with the therapist we went to, with her guidance and tools for us to learn how to reconnect after an argument, it became increasingly difficult for us to reconnect our souls. I took to therapy well and kept my word and my promises to him. I was in it 100 percent, a willing participant. Sadly, he could not control his fears. After a year of work, I knew if he left another time I would not go back. I could not do this anymore. The abandonment was too much. The therapy led me to heal and work on many deeper issues I had, including fear of love and commitment, but I was lost in a gut-wrenching battle with a tortured soul who couldn't keep his word. I was also in a battle of minds with my record label and Clive. I felt like both of my frontlines were under siege.

I had put body, mind, and soul into this relationship and if it couldn't work, even with the powerful tools we learned, it still wasn't working, there was nothing more I could do. I accepted the fate of the demise of the relationship and the rejection I would give him when he eventually came back to me. I knew I couldn't do this anymore. When I made my decision, I was at peace. It was all very clear to me, I knew I gave everything 100 percent. I couldn't love anyone more than I had. I couldn't do more than I was doing. So, there was nothing more to do. And that gave me a great sense of peace, revelation. Even though I knew I would suffer the loss, it was the end. You can give something everything you've got, and it still fails. There are no guarantees. That was a hard lesson for me to learn.

SOME WOULD SAY to take your time, take a breath between relationships, but that's not how I operated. Within two weeks I was out in the city with my crew at some club watching the gorgeous model Nick Scotti on stage, a discovery of Madonna going from model to popstar, having his shot at fame. It was during his show when I felt a hand on my back, and I turned around to see a handsome guy with a dazzling smile say, "Hi, your tag was out."

I looked at him and said, "Really?"

"Yes, but you're good now."

"Thanks, I'm Taylor."

"Hi, I'm Steven."

He was sitting down, and then he said, "I'm not that tall."

Huh?

That's when I realized what he meant. He was a model in a room packed with models to see Nick. I just laughed. What else could I do? Yup, he made me laugh. Just like that.

I was in the thick of New York Fashion Week, sitting front row for fashion shows of Todd Oldman to Anna Sui, even performing in one. Fashion, music, rock and roll, glamor, art.

I said, "Well, what kind of model are you if you're short?"

He said, "I do a lot of catalogs like Abercrombie and Fitch."

Was there an attraction? Sure, but after coming from such an intense relationship, laughter and easiness seemed the recipe, but at the same time it was like dating a boy. I fell right into the relationship. Steven would often come to the mansion now (as The Chef had) spending more time at my house, leaving little notes for me, which I thought were very sweet, even books from Dr. Seuss like *Oh, the Places We'll Go* and quotes from poets.

He had an adventurer spirit. He was into nature and weekend trips, not just staying at my house. *Let's go to Vermont. What are we doing this weekend?* He'd model all week doing catalog work for Macy's, Abercrombie and Fitch, and commercials, and we'd explore on the weekends, something I hadn't done with a partner before. Going to Maine, spending time in nature, in the city; I loved both worlds and we laughed a lot. I started to feel a lightness with him. It definitely wasn't the depth and intensity and desire

I had with The Chef, but I found I needed this as much as air. The adventures gave me a new feeling of freedom.

On an excursion to Vermont to see his property, he was no dummy, he knew I was a diva. When we get there, I'm looking at his property, but more than that, I'm looking for his house.

I said, "Where's the house?"

No, "I have land here. I'm gonna *build* a house. You want to stay here tonight?"

"In what, a fucking sleeping bag?" Yeah, uh, no.

"Ok, we'll go to my dad's."

I wasn't that immersed in being nature girl, but this was the beginning of a new era for me. The adventurous explorer. I started to understand how getting out of your own way and re-framing your thinking and physically putting your body into challenges could stop the negative thinking. I could get lost in the beauty, and one foot in front of the other, he turned me on to this world outside of my world. I loved it. This introduction to adventure, travel not for the sake of work but for the experience, led me into the physical beauty of nature and my need for it in my life.

Still deep into my third record and deeper into my troubles with Clive and with the label, Steven was almost a reprieve for me away from the mounting pressures. He showed me a different way of getting out of my head and I was very grateful. But his boy-like charm wasn't enough for me. I believed brooding and moodiness was normal in a relationship. I'd learned that from my father and I patterned that with The Chef. I started realizing that just because somebody seems deep doesn't mean they are. Maybe they are deeply full of shit or full of themselves. Just because it looks deep, doesn't mean the well goes very far down. That was another hard lesson to learn.

It was here that I realized relationships didn't need to be difficult or filled with angst. Being playful was also a needed part of a successful relationship because I knew I needed it. The adventures, the experiences getting into my physical body, hitting trailheads, enjoying friends at cookouts around my pool was a healthier way to feel. This felt right.

The combination of these experiences and the closeness of my friends, my family and his family and his friends was very healing, but with that playfulness and adventure, I didn't always take him seriously. I still attached angst and intensity to realness, complete unconscious thinking that lived within me. So when he would say, *I love you*, there was a part of me that just didn't believe it. I felt it was as easy as him saying, *Can I have a sandwich?*

We were having fun, so I was caught off guard when he said, "Honey, I love you, but this isn't working."

I was like, "What do you mean? Ok, I love you, too. I want to make this work."

He said, "It's too late. I got a booking in Australia and I will be gone for two months." He was going on to another adventure. I hadn't felt my way through all the hurt and disappointment and the wounds of my prior relationship. I was caught off guard. All the playfulness and all the adventure and all the learning had provided a safe place for me to forget and hide out. As he boarded the plane for Australia for a two-month photo shoot, I realized he was right. It wasn't working.

My manager told me, "You're young, you're beautiful, but you're tired." It was the first time I was accepting my limitations. At 29, I was very tired. I was both wise and foolish beyond my years. I was now a woman who needed to take care of herself and part of that was getting sleep, watching my diet, and exercising. Lisa (Diva 2 to my Diva 1) joined me and she went from 250 pounds down to 150 as she cooked and nurtured and took care of us following the advice and workout of my trainer. I took my manager's words to heart and we took care of ourselves spiritually, mentally, and physically.

Internally, I was crashing on fame and clashing with my label. Moneys being held up. Songs being remixed. Would the album ever be released? I was crumbling emotionally. I was no longer in any relationship. It seemed like those five years were hitting me hard. They had taken a toll. When you're at the top of the charts, everything seems great. Everyone is happy. But without that third record coming out, things started to slip. The music industry was slipping. Nobody likes to slip. I had pushed myself beyond my limits, and I was very hard on myself. I was a star, but I was a lonely star.

I was spending a shitload of money working with multiple producers and the one year to make a record turned into two as

Clive sent me back into the studio time and time again to recut and remix and spend more money that I would owe the record label ultimately.

Without a relationship to hide out in, I was more self-aware. I was world-aware. I was well-read. Conversations in my home ranged from dark to contentious to outright hilarious. I drove to the studio daily and usually came home to a group of people sitting around the pool. Lisa or Deborah or Leanne in the kitchen cooking. Lisa's mother on a train out from Brooklyn. The home was an LGBTQ/hetero safe haven for food, shelter, warmth, and to share your story.

Dr. Clarissa Pinkola Estés—*Women Who Run with the Wolves: Myths and Stories of the Wild Woman Archetype*—resonated with me and I gravitated to that mind set during this time. Was I a wild woman? What was I so desperately running to? Why wolves? How many so far? Who could say? But there was a part of me that needed that wildness. I found it very alluring and I was desperately attracted to it. I fell in love with the idea of being that Wild Woman, throwing it all away and running with the wolves. I felt passionate, powerful, innately creative, ageless, knowing and fertile. I was 30 years old.

Without a partner, I ached for the loss of my playmate in the landmines of doing remixes and changing songs on this never-ending recording process. I started to reach out to friends of mine who were just starting their lives while I was questioning mine. Some I went to high school with, they were beginning careers while I'd already been six years deep into mine. I took out the map of the United States and I thought, who's living where? What's a cool place where I can go get my adventure on and feel safe with some familiar crew nearby to explore the metaphor, the manifesto, so strong in my heart?

One of the first places I found myself in was New Mexico, Santa Fe specifically. My friend John from high school now studying at a wellness and massage center in this unique part of the country. I said, "I'm coming to visit but I will stay in a hotel nearby. Just spend the evening with me, don't disrupt your life. Let me know where good trailheads are. I'll meet you after work for food and drinks."

And so it began, my love affair with me, in Santa Fe. I rented a lovely *casita* right off Canyon Road. It was the month of December, I remember, because of the cold air, so crisp and fragrant with piñon and cedar. My senses were alive. I could do this on my own. My friends would tell me where the best trails were. I never asked them to take off work or babysit me. As a matter of fact, I never even wanted to stay with anybody. It was better. I felt this healing process for me. I needed to do it alone.

I traveled to Taos, San Francisco, Mill Valley, Mendocino, Big Sur, Boulder, Jackson Hole, and met friends nearby. I would map out two-, three-, four-, five-, six-mile hikes, going deep and deeper into the trails, deeper and deeper into a trance of meditation and prayer, one foot in front of the other, step by step. My relationship with nature, each step a step toward healing, losing the hurt and the pain, releasing and becoming one with my physical body and one with nature. Ultimately each step was a step with God. That was my prayer time. I used my body as a tool to take me there.

It was a time of self-reflection and self-discovery where my biggest problem was deciding where to hike for that day. I even snuck onto the Georgia O'Keefe estate to investigate. In Los Alamos, I explored the Indian Bandelier cliff dwellings and stood on mountaintops, just taking in the natural beauty and serenity, climbing higher, pushing my body, the fatigue a good sign. Then I turned my attention to Wyoming, traveling with friends to fish in the beautiful Snake River, sometimes catching 20 trout a day. Spending time with myself in the wild, in nature, in the philosophy of Henry David Thoreau, the philosophy of immersing yourself in the quiet, stripping away all your fears and roaming like the Native Americans did for thousands of years. I was a Jewish nomad. I felt that at some level, the nomadic nature deeply ingrained in my DNA connected me to God in a way I'd never been before. Imagine this period of my life; the freedom I was experiencing, the ability to go by myself for hours and miles, deep within the crevices of a mountain and paths and trails was in deep contrast to that girl who couldn't even leave home or get to a show without her boyfriend. I was now a safe zone for myself, and I was loving me.

I listened to the music of the trees, to the wind and deer, moose, and eagles as their wings spread and they swooshed off trees. I heard the world around me and connected back with mother earth, each moment another reflection, where I conquered my fear of being alone and made peace within.

At least once a year you'll find me breaking off for a unique adventure, a semi-challenge with myself and my comfort zone. Last year it was the Amazon with my children and exploring another world in another way, shared now with my kids, amongst kindred souls. This is what it feels like to be in a pack, right? I feel home when I'm in that space. Giving back to myself in this way has led me to heal greatly. Soon I'll probably go to Thailand, and I'll end up in a million Buddhist sanctuaries amidst the smell of night jasmine.

♭

WHY THE WOLF? Back in Santa Fe, I was driving down the mountain after a long hike as night was falling, no cars on this road, the snow falling hard in large clusters. My headlights landed on a creature slowly walking on the road 20 feet ahead of my car. I hit the brakes as my lights landed on the creature. It stopped in the middle of the road and stared at me with its big golden eyes and beautiful, full black coat. I knew right then and there in front of me was a full-grown wolf. We stared at each other. For a few moments no one moved. Then he slowly walked across the road and then loped up the embankment into the night of sagebrush and pinion. What a feeling! What a presence! In fact, I could feel the presence of everything. It was incredible. I said aloud, "Did I really see that? Taylor, did you see that?"

The next day I shared this with my friends, so excited, as they went to work and me to the Small Tesuque market for my morning breakfast burrito before I hit the trails. While reading the local newspaper and enjoying my meal, I came upon the livestock section of the classified ads. I saw the words "wolf puppies." WTF? I stopped and read, "Hybrid wolf puppies for sale." I knew right then and there it was no coincidence, and I needed one to come home with me. I immediately called the number in the paper and set up an appointment to drive the two hours to Dixon the next day to bring home a wolf puppy.

I was dating a cowboy from Dallas at the time who I had met a few weeks earlier in Vegas while I performed at the MGM. And somehow, I knew I would like Dennis to be my partner in this adventure and lay in my warm *casita*. I called him and asked him if he would like to join me in Santa Fe and go get a wolf puppy with me.

With Dennis driving and me shotgun, I felt good. Two hours turned to three as we got lost several times. It started getting dark which made it even more difficult to see where we were going as we passed small trailer parks tucked into the mountainside. We finally found the ranch that the woman on the phone had described "with cattle in the pasture and wolves on chains out front." What shocked us more as dusk fell hard was how she suddenly appeared at the car window looking like Kathy Bates in *Misery*. Fucking spooky. I think Dennis squealed a little with fright, but she was soothing to see in hat, boots, and parka because we were there. I asked, "Is this where the wolf puppies are?"

"Yes, come on, follow me."

We felt like we had entered the twilight zone, but I was determined. As the woman clunked her way down the driveway, we could barely see anything, but sure as shit as we drove closer to the barn, there out in the field were a few dogs. I saw an all-white, tall dog and realized that it was an arctic wolf. I could see a darker wolf near her. Dennis and I said nothing. We parked and got out of the car as she said, "Come with me." We walked towards the barn, and there was nobody else around. And as we entered a sparse room, she said, "All right, bring them out."

From behind a door out walks the face of an angel, a boy about ten years old, a beautiful, biracial child holding three puppies. I whispered to Dennis, "There's no fucking way that kid's hers." He heard me loud and clear.

In the boy's arms the three wolf pups. He said, "I have two more," and he brought them out. One was very light with a white heart face, the lightest of them and the fattest. The others were quite dark, grayish. Two were black and all had amber eyes.

I didn't know what to ask, so I said like you would to any breeder, "Can I see the parents? Is the mother here?"

She said, "Yes. Bring in the parents."

I asked Dennis, "You're supposed to see the parents, right?"

"I think so," he said.

With a huff she said, "I'm going to bring in the arctic."

As we heard a loud noise banging from next door in the barn a man said, "Mother!" Dennis and I looked at each other as the boy still stood next to us with the puppies in his arms.

She said, "Father, we're going to go get the female." Then she turned to me. "They're from a sanctuary. They're research wolves."

"Oh." I didn't really know how to respond. The woman under the hat was clearly white. The boy was biracial, and we never saw who belonged to the voice in the other room called "father." She couldn't be the mother of this child, could she? The boy had a calming presence as he patiently stood there. I wondered, *Should I say something? Do I intervene?* The woman walked in with one wolf—white as white, long and tall, lanky, almost thin. She said, "This is the mother. She's full arctic." We were staring at a wolf. This was not a dog. Its eyes amber as any amber could be. She goes, "Father, we're going to bring in the male." The boy was still holding the puppies. We found out they were only three weeks old. Normally you never take a puppy from a mother until eight weeks, but I knew we needed to leave with the dog because we were certainly never coming back up this way again.

When the male was brought in, I said, "Aren't these hybrids?"

She said, "Well, some of them have a little malamute in them."

If anybody's ever done their homework on wolves, the more north the breed—a malamute, a Husky—they're basically direct descendants of wolves. I didn't see much malamute. I saw a male timber wolf, the larger of most wolf breeds because of the game they feed on. I said, "OK." Being illegal to sell a full-bred wolf, I had to ask again, "I thought these were hybrids."

She said again, "They probably have a little malamute in them."

As she took the male out, I looked at the boy and said, "Which puppy do you like?"

He said softly, "I like this one. I like him most. He's the biggest. I spend the most time with him."

We decided that would be the pup. As the lady went to the house, I turned to the boy in one little desperate attempt and said, "Are you okay? Are you okay if we leave?"

He didn't say anything at first. He turned away. Then said, "I'm alright. I'm okay." He looked like an angel, like Gabriel, the Messenger of God.

I said, "Should we call somebody? Can we leave you here?" I truly believed this kid was abducted.

Dennis and I paid her $200, said our goodbyes and hugged this dear child. We took our newfound puppy named Tikan, which Kelly Cutrone told me meant "spirit of wolf" in Sioux that she learned from her close friend, John Trudell, the Native American activist. We took Tikan into our casita and hugged and held all three weeks of him. Tikan went on to spend the next nine years with me as my wild man.

Eventually I took him back to my Long Island home where he had acres to roam and get into a whole lot of mischief once I got him housebroken. He was my live-in partner in crime. I tried to keep him on my property with electric fencing, but with his three layers of fur he'd hop over it like a gazelle and go mess around with the Polo ponies in the barn at the state park. He'd take the time to roll in every bit of feces and dead animal he could find before coming home to show me a story. One time he came home with a hoof mark on his head. Nothing kept this wolf on my property. People would ask what I fed him, like I threw him raw meat. He ate dog food. He was just a gorgeous specimen. Tikan loved walks on the nature trail. He was my man. He was my wild man.

Was he a pet? Was he my dog? One hundred percent. Was he dog-like? Well, not really. He looked like a husky meets a Great Dane with his long-ass legs. Any man who came into my house was scared when he saw Tikan. He was very quiet until they got too close to him. His growl would turn into a menacing snarl if you got too close and cornered him. Always made me chuckle.

FAME AND RECOGNITION had led me to seek my wholeness and peace in the wilderness. My mom had her teachings with her guru at the ashram. After their separation, even my father had to come to terms with his past. He no longer had a captive audience to feed the rage that flowed through his body. He felt he had no choice but to get therapy and go inside. And I was happy for him.

My sabbatical helped put things into perspective for me. Tensions with Clive were driving a wedge between me and the record company. The album was coming on the heels of big personal growth of a 31-year-old woman of independent thinking. I needed to push through and challenge my own creativity. My own restrictions weighed heavily on me like a child that I needed to birth. This album didn't come out until 1993, three years between records. That's a long time in the pop world. Keeping your fans interested and engaged, not losing momentum, it's difficult to keep the machine cranking and the star in place.

The music sounds were changing as well. R&B was dominating charts with TLC, En Vogue, Brownstone, Aaliyah, and Maxwell. Then there were bands like Nirvana and Pearl Jam, raw rock coming out of Seattle.

I'd also found the strength to change management, no longer with Champion. I was working with Frank Dileo, but I kind of felt nomadic. I felt unmanaged on some level. I was soon on a management merry-go-round. So many changes were taking place in the industry. Managers were becoming executives at record labels, continuing the blurred lines and muddy waters between lawyers and artist and executives. Labels like LaFace and Bad Boy were breaking. One month someone had a management company, the next they are the CEO of Sony.

As I worked on more songs and shot videos that were rejected, my financial debt to the label continued to grow. Clive said "no" more often than "yes" to the music I was putting together. Since I wasn't on tour, I wasn't getting paid. That didn't stop mortgage payments, that didn't stop the mounting bills. Being in debt never stopped a bill from coming in. I was becoming more overwhelmed with the financial aspects of my life. It became clear to me that I could no longer support a mansion with $25,000 a month in bills and maintenance as my debt to the record company grew.

Selling the house in 1995 felt like a relief. I sold the mansion and moved out farther to a secluded, smaller house on five acres in an area of Lloyd Harbor called "The Neck." I wanted time and space between me and the world. I needed a buffer. The property backed up to 2,500 magical acres of protected land so it was very private. With plenty of nature available to me to get lost in, I spent a lot of time walking and soul searching with my wolf. I enjoyed being immersed in nature and the small community, but at the same time I was unintentionally isolating myself.

The record was coming together. I worked with Shep Pettibone (who had worked with Madonna), Clivilles & Cole of C+C

Music Factory, and Narada Michael Walden—all top producers. The songs written during this period of time were "I'll Wait" (about my relationship with The Chef), "Send Me a Lover," "Can't Get Enough of Your Love," "Say a Prayer" (another song I wrote), "Dance with a Stranger," "I Could Be Good for You" (the first single), "Soul Dancing" (the title track), "The Door to Your Heart," "Someone Like You," "Memories," and "If You Were Mine." In total, I co-wrote six of the tracks. I felt triumphant on one level and drained on the next. I had my manager Frank in my corner, but he kept saying "don't push Clive."

Sitting on set to produce the first video, we waited for Clive to decide which song we were going to shoot. I'd already done the video for "I'll Wait" with Matthew Rolston, an amazing photographer who I put in the director chair as a lot of artists were doing, but Clive ultimately dismissed that video. Now with Randee St. Nicholas at the helm, my choreographer and dancers on set, everyone was waiting on Clive to decide between "Can't Get Enough of Your Love" or my co-write "I'll Wait." Hours passed, and money was wasted. Of course, I wanted my single to be first, but inevitably, he chose the remake of Barry White's hit. After Whitney's "I'm Every Woman" (with C+C), he felt this was the best way to go for the first single. It was a hit, even internationally in Italy, Australia, and Canada. The second single Clive chose was "Send Me a Lover." It only went as high as Top Twenty. Finally, my single "I'll Wait" was released.

Setting up the tour to support *Soul Dancing* was the only place I was going to see any money. Making that record wasn't a particularly pleasant experience, and it put me in a large amount of debt to the record company. Joe was once again my road manager. We were rehearsing for a couple of days in New Orleans before the tour. We were in the hotel where I was reading my latest book while my background singers, Jenny and Vivian, were glued to the television. We were waiting for Terri when Joe called and said she wasn't on her plane.

On TV another drama was unfolding, a white Ford Bronco was slowly driving on a California highway followed by a ton of police cruisers and helicopters. It was the OJ Simpson chase. Joe kept coming in with updates on Terri. He still hadn't been able to locate her. I was focused on my book, the girls on the TV, and

Joe on searching for Terri.

As Joe, the sensible one, became more agitated, I knew something bad was happening, not only on TV where it seemed the world was changing, but also around me. One day turned to two days, and by the time we tracked her down, the unimaginable had occurred. Terri been beaten within an inch of her life by the man she loved, someone I'd met briefly. This tragedy affected us in a deep way. This was my soul sister, my winger, yet I was committed to dates on the road and I couldn't be there for her.

We tried to make sense of the violence as she lay in the hospital with a metal plate in her head. When I finally had an opportunity to speak with her, she was a shadow of her former self. The violence had taken hold of her. She wasn't the spirited Terri in her heart. When she spoke, I heard a vacancy in her voice. She seemed removed. Very slowly, she said, "I can't go back out on the road, T. I can't."

I was devastated. We'd lost a member of the family. She was gone just like that. When you're out there traveling, you are each other's family. These are the people you rely on day in and day out. These are the ones you share your happy news with, the births, the celebrations, as well as the pain and the sorrow. Between tours, she had her own life, with her children and her mother. She would sing background for other groups like Guns & Roses and Mötley Crüe to support her family. We kept in touch during the downtime, but it just never occurred to me that she was in this kind of trouble. It broke my heart. She moved further away from us and immersed herself in the Seven-Day Adventist Church, leaving the music business entirely.

A sadness grew within me on the road without her there. I had the rest of my tour family, but it felt like me against the world. For some reason I felt isolated, like I did in my secluded home. It was Terri who had helped me navigate the initial craziness and the fame. She had been my buffer between the roughness and rawness of Odessa to my first tour, my first everything. I'll never forget having to sing with BeBe and CeCe Winans on their Christmas TV special, and Terri said, "When you sing 'Amazing Grace,' drag it out real slow. Child, you got this, but you need to take your time." I started over from the beginning. "No, no, no, no, no! Make the word 'amazing' last 10 seconds." I'd never thought of it that way. After my performance, BeBe and CeCe said, "Taylor, you're remarkable. What church are you from?" That was Terri's love and guidance over me. I missed her, but I had an album to promote. I was reminded daily that I had a job to do and bills to pay. My tour continued, but it was never the same without her.

In 1996, when the call came in to Ric that we should do a Greatest Hits record, I was stunned. I was surprised. I was shocked. My fourth record will be a Greatest Hits? True to form, Ric said, "What can we do? This is what Clive wants." Arista was doing the same thing with their other acts. It was a way for them to hit their earnings numbers. TLC, Toni Braxton, Expose, Taylor Dayne—we were all expected to produce a Greatest Hits album. Trouble was, with no new songs and usually no touring income, there was very little financial compensation for the artist. It was a business decision. As a result, several groups filed for bankruptcy protection.

My *Greatest Hits* album contained fourteen tracks, all of the favorites and even a couple of remixes to generate interest among fans who already had those songs in their collection. They even released an updated version of "Say a Prayer" as a single. Around that time, I also had hit songs included on movie soundtracks like *Fried Green Tomatoes*, *The Shadow*, and *The Secret Garden*.

Ric said he had an attorney who could get me out of my Arista deal and I could get signed to A&M. "How can we do that?" I asked. It was an answer I didn't want to hear. The plan was for me to file bankruptcy, just like those other groups had, so that I could be released from my contract. I felt like Ric would have my back although so much has transpired between us. It was a confusing time and I didn't know which deals benefitted who anymore. More blurred lines.

Going through bankruptcy was a long, drawn-out process. There was the filing, the negotiations, the legal review, and on and on. As my case snaked its way through the legal system, Ric said he had a production deal with A&M. Once the smoke cleared, and I was no longer with Arista, Ric immediately signed me to his deal at A&M records. Then we were back in the studio putting music together, and within six months I was dropped from A&M. I'll never know what was truly going on and who it served, definitely not me. Having left Arista as a platinum-selling artist, why would I be dropped so quickly? It broke my heart, but the damage was done. I felt defeated with no label in place and nowhere to release my music.

By 1997, I had no label deal as the internet took the music world by storm, sharing music in a way no one had ever heard of. Napster.

## CHAPTER 6
# Out Here on My Own

Perseverance. Strength. A strength that comes from somewhere deep inside you. Often through our own vulnerabilities our strength is tested through loss. Part of that is just resilience and holding on tight to that light that still has some spark left in me.

Looking back on my musical journey, I know there are things I could have done differently, but I'd like to think that my personal resilience and persistence helped open the door and keep it open for young female artists who came after me who had something to say. Women who have since fought similar battles and won. No doubt I was the cautionary tale told in many a room on more than a few occasions. Female artists pack a powerful punch in our business. Platforms like *The Voice, American Idol, X Factor,* and social media and digital streaming have given the artist the ability to connect directly with the audience to market and promote themselves.

It wasn't just me who was having a hard time with the industry. It was epidemic. Prince was speaking out against Warner Brothers, refusing to uncover his face on TV and appearing on-stage with the word SLAVE written on his cheek to demonstrate how the music industry mistreated artists. George Michael had an epic fight with Sony. Same with Michael Jackson. Then there was the Milli Vanilli lip-synching scandal. The status quo was crumbling from vinyl to cassettes to CDs and the evolution of MTV and VH1 away from continuous music videos.

I'd ridden the wave as one of the hottest stars of the late '80s and early '90s. Now a new form of music sharing, digital streaming, was taking control, and the music labels had no idea how to control it. As I was facing all this uncertainty and opportunity under the scrutiny of a label that didn't love me back, my management wasn't very strong and consistent at all. That left me feeling very alone with big decisions to make. Everyone having conflicts of interests and too many hands in the pie.

Mostly I knew that what my heart felt was different from what "they" wanted, which was to disregard my own instincts and remind me daily they owned me. It was The Wild Woman in me that said, *no more*, as I felt a noose was being held over my head, and I had nowhere to go but through the rabbit hole.

I did what I had to do to break away from Arista. Guided by lawyers who had their own agendas, and parties with conflicts of interest. Arista had two other bankruptcy filings going on as well as mine with Toni Braxton and TLC. During that time, mine didn't end gracefully. Promised a record deal with another major label, I was immediately signed and dropped within six months. I began a period of real soul searching and career choices that led to some big decisions. It was a scary time, as I settled into the idea of being on my own. Being the captain of my own ship was almost a relief as I felt a sense of peace with it. Letting go...

I'd always regretted letting that role in *Married to the Mob* slip through my fingers, in 1987, not having a manager to even follow up with opportunities like this. I probably wouldn't have been able to fit it into my crazy schedule those first two years of my career, but what if I'd done it!

During my press and promotion for the last record I released with Arista, I did a live appearance on *The Tonight Show with Jay Leno*. The next day I got a call from my theatrical agent saying Warren Beatty had seen me on the show. He wanted to meet with me about a film he was casting to star alongside his new wife Annette Benning, the actress he met and married after they starred in *Bugsy*.

I was told the film was a remake of the classic *Love Affair*. Warren would like to call me to discuss a role. I was on tour and in a hotel room in the middle of Europe under my alias, Miss Ruby Love.

"Hi, it's Warren."

"Hi, Warren."

"Hi there. Do you always go under the alias Miss Love?"

"Yes, I like how it sounds when they call my room and say my name to me."

He said, "Julie used to use the name Ruby, too. You remind me of a young Julie Christie."

Warren said this! I held the phone up and away from my face, staring at it, shocked. Yep, I was straight-up blushing, from six thousand miles away! He got me good. I was beyond excited that my first major film appearance would be in a Warren Beatty movie. Thank you, God.

Here I am feeling pushed out of the music business where I dominated for years, selling millions of records, and then at 32 years old asking, *Is my career over?* And out of the blue here was the King of film looking to work with me. That felt more than good.

Working on that movie was a great experience that took over a year to film, unusual to say the least, with a big budget and big actors—Warren Beatty, Annette Benning, Garry Shandling, Katherine Hepburn, and Chloe Webb. Warren was the most charming, brilliant man. He was always so complimentary. He'd say, "I was just so blown away by your performance. You're beautiful and real." That kindness really helped because I was in the middle of a major movie and I was never more nervous in my life. I'd be sitting in the trailer, and he'd come by after filming and say, what do you think about this? What do you think about that? Would you say it like this? I was thinking, *this is insane*. This is Warren Beatty asking me how I would write my part in a scene? God it felt so good just to be asked.

Like anything else I put my mind to, I knew I had to work hard and research and get more hours under my belt and that meant practice. I took classes. Working an acting muscle was not something I had done before, so I needed to exercise it, learn it, and practice, thinking and hearing differently. Just the way I'd learned to really listen to music, I trained myself to focus on dialogue, to study human interactions. I learned to memorize lines and live truthfully in imaginary circumstances as my teacher taught me. I listened so I could take in the information and apply it to the new work. I was up for the challenge. It's also easier to go all in when you don't have much to lose.

During the sporadic filming of *Love Affair*, I kept auditioning and working and touring on weekend warrior shows for income. I landed a lead role in an independent film, and it was a demanding role. The movie was called *Stag*, an HBO film about a stag party that takes a deadly turn when one of the strippers is accidentally killed by one of the men in attendance. I played the other stripper, the one who lives, the one who makes those men pay for what they did to my friend. It was an intense experience, and I had to hold my own among a group of impressive actors like Ben Gazzara, Mario Van Peebles, Jerry Stiller, Andrew McCarthy, and Kevin Dillon. All men and me. It filmed in New York in a house in Long Island, so my little home was often the hangout after hours. It was a hell of a way to immerse myself into the moviemaking process. A three-week shoot at full-tilt boogie.

Soon, I was in the groove and living the actor life—studying, taking meetings, and going out for pilot season in LA—and it was paying off. I got signed to Gallin/Morey Management. I had a powerful company behind me, and I finally felt that professionally there was someone in my corner.

That gave me the confidence I needed. I did several TV pilots and a few TV movies like *NightMan* and *Jackie's Back*. I had a good role in a film called *Fool's Paradise*, and then landed a recurring role on a new scripted series for Showtime called *Rude Awakenings*. It was the premium cable network's first foray into producing their own scripted series. I worked hard for that role and got it. The cast was made up of seasoned performers, just like the *Stag* movie, and I held my own. The other actors included Lynn Redgrave, Sherilyn Fenn, Richard Lewis, Tim Curry, and even Roger Daltrey.

I got a call from my management that Roseanne's people had offered me a lead recurring role, a four-month commitment to film the series and flip the switch on their TV marriage. That was all the invitation I needed to go west. The rest would come.

The move to LA was to be a temporary one to shoot the TV series. Up until that time I was living in the smaller house out on The Neck with my wolf and much younger boyfriend, Wolfboy. He was 22 to my 32, and we had met through our veterinarian. He had a wolf/dog as well. We bonded immediately over hybrids and chemistry. It was a challenging relationship, yet we managed to be together on and off for two years.

I wasn't sure about him relocating with me even temporarily because I didn't think he could handle the move or leaving Long Island. I knew I would miss him, but he said he wanted to come. And he did, by driving our dogs from NY to LA in a packed car while I flew. I was doing shows on the west coast and getting our hippie palace off Lookout Mountain and Laurel Canyon into shape. He lasted three weeks. One morning he packed up his car, took his dog, and left, I assumed to drive back to New York. Just like that.

A week later, feeling sick, nauseous, depressed, and lonely, and needing help, I dragged myself to a doctor. Blood tests were taken. The shocker? I was pregnant! HTF? I had doubted I could even get pregnant, and I'd made peace with that. Still, here I was with child and almost ten weeks pregnant! I was blindsided. I had no idea. But it definitely started to make sense, how sick and overwhelmed I was feeling. Now with this new information, I became more depressed and confused.

I needed someone to help me. I needed love and guidance. I needed to unload the weight I felt. I found a spiritual guide, a recommended channeler. I asked her, "How was this possible? I didn't think I could get pregnant." I told her my story and my sadness. She said, "This child will wait for you—if you cannot—if it is too much to bear being alone and you can't meet her now, she understands, and she will wait for you. Her name is Astaria."

The room stopped. Astaria! Yes! I knew it in my bones. I always knew I would have a girl. I thought for years I would name her Isis after the Bob Dylan song on his album *Desire* about his beautiful girl.

When she said, "Her soul will wait for you," my heart stopped. I felt my mind settle and I began to wail. I. Let. Go. I had reached out. I needed a sign. I needed love, and I got it through this woman. I was met by the universe. My "hope flame" was still alive, that little speck of light was still there, burning in my soul, a small ember that began to glow brighter the moment I heard those words.

The endless sorrow that had lived in my bones the last few weeks stilled. I felt lighter. I took a deep breath. A different picture appeared before me now, one that was hopeful. The doubt and guilt I carried with me was replaced with a seed of hope and certainty and comfort. I wasn't alone. I made a decision. I knew what I had to do.

Making a choice like that is difficult at any age. Me being in my early thirties, it was just devastating. I experienced a mountain of emotions after the procedure. It was a surreal time for me, and the one thing that helped me center myself and not fall deeper into a depression was returning to therapy and going back into a daily practice of healing. I was going to group therapies (like Al-Anon), a social and healing group for me. The tools were there in the room and sharing with strangers over our similar feelings and circumstances at meetings helped me a lot. Living in a new city, it gave me a place to go daily and share, gain strength in numbers and some clarity over my loss while moving slowly forward.

I also knew I needed more assistance this time. I was in new territory, literally by myself, in a house in the hills with my wolf. So, when a friend recommended I see a psychiatrist, as I was in a daily fight with myself to get out of bed and out the door, I really had no good reason not to.

A psychiatrist. It was a first for me. Now 33 years old, I went and after five minutes of him hearing me describe my feelings and situation, he prescribed an antidepressant (Zoloft) and a plan. I walked away with my script and followed the doctor's orders. I needed help with the double punch of losses that I'd experienced in love and life. After a week, I was feeling a bit better, combined with daily hikes along the numerous trails and paths I was discovering through the Hollywood Hills, along with therapy, yoga, and some new friendships I was developing. I began to feel the sun on my face and feelings of overwhelming gratitude.

After the four months were up, I felt no rush to go back to NY. I renewed my rental lease but did it LA style, month to month. I then went ahead and rented out my house in Long Island. I was in no rush to go back there and feel those feelings.

I still had my apartment in NYC, so when I wanted to go back, I could. And over time I did go back to work and see my family and friends and to be in the city, but I never lived there permanently again. I was enjoying my new life in LA: the sunny days, the warmth surrounding myself with other women in the music and entertainment industry of all ages, having a more integrated and healthier lifestyle than the one I had in NY. Most people were bi-coastal or NY transplants, so it was easier to develop friendships. I had new adventures and new lovers and was now in the thick of Hollywood as I opened my heart up to the west coast.

The entertainment industry is filled with stories of near misses and opportunities that slip through your fingers; that's part of the bigness, films get made and never released; actors filming huge scenes and roles only to be cut out entirely and left on the editing floor. TV shows were dropped and not picked up for another season.

In *Roseanne*, I was cast to play the woman who John Goodman "Dan" falls in love with, and he leaves Roseanne. It was one of the highest-rated series for years, so I couldn't believe when it was pulled from the network. Unimaginable. The show was canceled before I even got in front of a camera.

It was disappointing to be sure, but I saw it through and remained friends with Roseanne, who ultimately went on to do her own talk show that I was on a year later. She also introduced me to Leah Remini, a brilliant funny actress starring on *The King of Queens*, and who became a close friend.

One time when Roseanne, Leah, and I went out to dinner, Roseanne was describing the things she could do with a ping-pong ball. Leah chiming in, "No fucking way I'm doing any of that with a ping-pong ball!" We were loud, funny, and successful. They were two completely unapologetic woman before me, and it was a refreshing change from the picture-perfect veneer that passes for sincerity in LA. Admitting to living in California and loving it for a New Yorker is like saying out loud "NY pizza sucks!" It ain't gonna happen! I mean I will always be a New Yorker, but I loved LA.

Over the years I did more video shoots, TV appearances, and award shows in LA, yet I hadn't recorded music there. Now with new management on the west coast and with time on my hands, I started thinking about making music. I was encouraged to do so as I started to digest the changes in my life from NY to LA in a big way. I was set up in creative sessions with new producers and writers, and soon I had an independently financed record in the works. Creatively it was an enjoyable time for me, and by 1998 I was holding the reins of my career.

But be careful what you wish for. Now I was the label. As with everything in my life I have ever set my intention on, this was no different. It was a challenge I couldn't turn away from. I dug in, rolled up my sleeves, and got my hands dirty, keeping my eyes on the prize.

What an undertaking, from concept to collaborations with writers, producers, musicians, A&R, studios, budgets. It was intense, and incredibly rewarding because I was watching my own vision materialize. But like building your dream home, it's not something I would take on again.

Yet this opportunity to make music again was huge. Working with a new team of writers and producers, I was able to take all the loose ends I had felt with my rapid departure from the music industry and give it an outlet. All my mixed feelings went into making that record. And once I got into it, I found my rhythm and I made the decisions for better or worse. The transition from music into acting, relocating, the loss of a child and a relationship, I was now beginning to understand what it really felt like to live unapologetically.

The album *Naked Without You* was my fourth baby, my fourth birth. I co-wrote, produced and A&R'ed the record. I co-wrote seven of the songs. The tracks were "Don't Make Me Love You," "Whenever You Fall," "Unstoppable," "Naked Without You," "Whatever You Want," "Stand," "You Don't Have to Say You Love Me," "Love's Gonna Be On Your Side," "Dreams," "There Is No Heart That Won't Heal," "Soon As My Heart Breaks," and "Whatever you Want/Remix. "

The record released in 1998 on Neptune Records/Platinum Entertainment (Neptune was my label). We released three singles: "Unstoppable," "Naked Without You," and "Whatever You Want," a song I'd written a few years earlier for my last Arista project that Clive had passed on. Tina Turner then went on to record my song and made it a smash.

I knew that working with an independent label would be different. I wouldn't have the same level of funds, distribution, and reach with marketing and promotion dollars, and I would have a limited staff. *Naked Without You* hit the billboard charts into the top 200, nowhere near my past success. Yet, the single remix "Naked Without You" (Thunderpuss 2000 club mix) went #1 on the Billboard Dance charts. It was a smaller victory and I had to learn to downsize my expectations and honor the effort and achievement.

Even the photoshoot was done with care. I brought on Bert Stern, the famous photographer of Marilyn Monroe's last sitting of nudes. I needed to push the envelope and take my image in a new direction. I wanted to show myself raw, naked, exposed. I was no expert in graphics and layout and I always look at that cover and say "I wish..." Despite that, it was still an accomplishment I was anxious to share with my fans.

The same music execs were still around and one I met with for TV and film syncs was like, "Yeah, Taylor, I like the new stuff. It's good but listen to this. This is great!"

He wasn't wrong. The album was *The Miseducation of Lauryn Hill*, who had been a singer in the Fugees, and was the voice under their "Killing Me Softly." Here she made her solo debut into history. Her song "Ex-factor" will forever be in my top 10 list. A perfect musical storm took over and she rode that wave like a tsunami. I felt left behind.

By the year 2000, musical tastes had made Britney Spears a superstar along with boy bands like NSync. Rap and hip-hop with Run DMC, Snoop to Biggie, Dre and P Diddy, and the Beastie Boys were taking center stage along with neo-soul superstars like D'Angelo, who changed the musical game with his drop of "How Does It Feel" as well as Erykah Badu and Maxwell.

My relationships were rolling along, in Hollywood, out most nights, returning to music, and touring. I was dating an actor who was very well known for his past relationships, good looks, and for losing his temper in bars he partly owned from NY to Miami to LA. I loved all 6' 3" of John and his hard teddy bear heart. We traveled together often, and it was during our relationship that I really began thinking about having a baby. John was into the idea as well and we kinda tried, knowing now I could get pregnant. Now at 36, my clock was ticking.

It was late 2000 when I was asked by Disney to come to NY and star in the musical *Aida* with music by Elton John and Tim Rice. The catch? It was a one-year commitment. I was very familiar with the musical as I was an original cast member with Audra McDonald and Sheri Rene Scott. I did two three-week workshops for Disney's Katzenberg and Elton and Tim and other execs to see their process live and do rewrites. A long process, it is.

Four years later, now a hit on Broadway, this was an opportunity clearly to consider. But one year back in NY in my apartment? That's a commitment. Broadway is not for the weary with eight shows a week. I gave it great thought, back in LA hanging with BFF Jenny M. She also was currently living in my pseudo-guesthouse out back with no bathroom and peeing in a kiddie pool if she really had to go in the middle of night.

When I told Jenn about the NY possibility and other random things as girlfriends/roommates do, I said, "Hey, I was thinking about getting lipo."

She looks at me and says, "Yeah, me too, let's do it!"

I'm like WTF? Seriously, you're a perfect ten! This girl had the body of a goddess. Didn't matter. If I was getting it, she was getting it, too. I said, "Jenn, you don't need it."

She says, "You don't need it either." Fine.

Fast-forward to the doctor performing the procedure in his surgical center with Jenn and me going under a haze of drugs. Jenn was in the next room insisting she go that same day. One minute we're laughing and chatting across the hall, high as kites, and the next I'm looking up at the ceiling slowly coming out of anesthesia. My vision blurred. I thought I saw faces above me. But as I gained focus, the faces formed into children, all smiling and looking at me. I got a little emotional and didn't realize it, but I said out loud, "I want a baby."

"So, have one," a voice said somewhere in the room.

"Huh? Have a baby?" I looked around and spotted her. I said, "How? I'm not married. I have no real boyfriend."

She said, "So what? Rent a womb, child. That's what I did and look at all them babies up there."

I asked for details. Later I couldn't remember a goddamn thing she said I was so groggy and high. But I remembered how it made me feel, hopeful, as she told me about her surrogacy and how it was an alternative to carrying a child. Which she couldn't do. My thoughts went wild. "What does the baby look like?" This was new territory for me.

I mean, the pictures on display were her kids, beautiful and smiling. She was a proud South American queen from Trinidad who was the head nurse and married to the doctor. Both were deep in their 40s with her unable to conceive. I got what she was saying, but she was definitely black, and he was defiantly white. So, what was the race of the surrogate?

She said, "Child, it looks like you! I'm black, my husband is white and it's ours. My surrogate was white, but it don't matter. It's your egg, child. It looks like you! I used my egg, and my husband's sperm. We put our embryos in her. You rent a womb, child, literally." That was some heavy shit for a little girl who was wearing adult diapers about to be wheeled out to her car.

When we were leaving, I told her I would be calling her for more info, and I did. I also did some of my own research and found out the process was only legal in the state of California and one other state; Delaware, I think. This was the year 2000 so there were only a small number of agencies doing this type of practice. And if you were a single parent or a gay unmarried couple, it was next to impossible to get taken on as a client. I searched around and finally got accepted and put on a waiting list with a wonderful agency. I wrote a check to reserve my place and just like that I had a plan. Otherwise, what was this all for?

My plan was to be in NYC for rehearsals six months later. By then hopefully I'd have a surrogate on board and we would start the fertility process. I could fly back to LA on dark days (no play performance) if need be for the transfer while the surrogate stays in LA and gets pregnant and goes to term with my healthy baby. It takes about a year. That sounded sane to me.

After my breakup with John, I was on my own a few months with the wind knocked out of my sails. Now with the decisions of leaving for a year, my biggest concern and hardest decision to make was who would be the sperm donor? Did I want a baby daddy? No, I didn't think so at that point. I felt now I could do this on my own, but with who? Who could I trust? Should I just go to the sperm bank? Not quite as sophisticated a solution as it is today. This was eighteen years ago. No photos, just good blood and high IQ and guaranteed healthy.

For me, I didn't want a faceless donor. I wanted to have some connection, at least something shared. My head and my heart searched and kept coming back to one guy from my past. Manchild. Our relationship fizzled over time and distance with our age difference. He was twenty and I was six years older. But we had maintained a true love for one another, and he had the utmost respect for me. Over the years we hooked up a few times, and at this point, Manchild was a 30-year-old man.

So, I called him. I pretty much got to the point quickly, "Hi, hon, what's up? Would you consider giving me a special gift? A donation of love?" Jesus, I sounded too weird. "Would you think about being a sperm donor for me to try and have a child?" I rambled on, assuring him that he wouldn't be financially responsible in any way and he could be involved as much or as little as he wanted to be, emotionally and physically. What can I say? I trusted him.

He waited a moment and then said, "Darling, this is a lot to take in. Can I meet you in NY in two days to talk in person?"

"Of course!"

This man got on a plane, showed up at my apartment, looked me in the eyes, and said, "Taylor, at 19 years old you changed my life. I trusted you then, and I trust you now. Yes, I would be honored to father a child for you." A beautiful man.

My master plan was in motion. I always believed. Build it and they will come. Success is when preparation meets opportunity. Follow the yellow brick road. Fall off the horse, get back on. Five months later I received a call from the agency. A surrogate was available in the next couple of weeks. It was January 2001.

In February, I landed in New York to play Amneris in Disney's Broadway production of Elton John and Tim Rice's *Aida*. I'm here to tell you, theatre is not for the weak. Broadway demands 100% of your physical, vocal, and emotional being, week after week. I took my closing bow, happily exhausted, on September 8, 2001. I was ready to return to LA to nest while awaiting the birth of my children. Packing up my apartment that week, Jenny M. was in NY with me for my final shows and to help me after I was to have boob surgery the morning of September 10th. There was no way I was gonna be a mom and not look good! LOL!

The next morning, September 11th, with a nurse in my apartment and Jenny getting coffee for the nurse and herself at 8:45 a.m. while I slept, the world changed. Living on 15th and 5th Ave, Jenn was at LePain on 5th when the first plane hit. All traffic stopped; all the cabs and buses and vehicles were still as they witnessed the smoke and the fire.

The TV was on in the apartment, our phones were getting spotty reception, and the nurse's husband was in one of the towers! She was in such shock she couldn't remember his phone number. The city was mayhem and national security, tanks, choppers, fire and police cars were everywhere. Her husband, thank God, made it out on a lower floor and ran to my apartment. He called her, as he ran with hundreds, from the fires and debris and smoke filling the air, running as the buildings began to collapse.

I was not in good shape, but when her husband got to us, you could feel what he just witnessed and survived. He was a shadow of a man badly shaken, covered in a weird yellowish ash. He never really spoke, just sat there and stared as the TV continued to show details day and night of what was happening outside my window.

For two days, no one was allowed in or out of the city, no transit. We were holed up in my one-bedroom apartment, not forced to evacuate as I was above the 14th Street cutoff. We tried to make calls to get out of the city. We tried calling friends to make sure no one was hurt, but we were cut off from the rest of the world. It became more real as the devastation continued. We didn't have much contact for two days. The nurse spent time with her husband and took care of me as well. I now had no doctor to return to for my post-op checkup since all surgeons were now on call at the hospitals taking in the injured.

By day three, people were getting through from out of state. A call came in from my surrogate. "I've been trying to get a hold of you." I did my best to reassure her. I told her that I was okay in NY. She said, "Are you sitting down?" I didn't know what to say. I couldn't bear more loss.

She said, "No, I have wonderful news! We—You are having a girl! You're having a boy and a girl! OMG! A true miracle!" *Her soul will wait for you, for the right time...*

I had found out in early June that the surrogate was pregnant. Ten days later, with twins! Wanting to know the sex, I made my first flight to LA while working in *Aida*. Three months later I went back to do the amnio and ultrasounds and see her.

I saw what the doctors saw, I was having twin *boys*. The doctors tried to convince me, and the proof was there, but I never bought it. I had such belief I was having my girl again. Never forgetting the sage words of the channeler, that I would meet my daughter one day in the future. She was right all along. And on that day, clutching the phone in my little apartment knowing of all the souls who had just left their bodies one mile from me, I knew her soul had waited to come back. When we were finally able to leave New York, I went home to LA to reconnect with my surrogate and soon-to-be-born twins. A son and a daughter.

The kids were due early January. I had one nanny in place, and one that was a possibility but not a done deal. My assistant told me she had a friend named Benita who was leaving her job at the Post Office and was looking for work.

"She's already got three granddaughters, so she's had lots of practice."

"Of course she does. The laws of sisterhood!"

"I'm telling you, she can raise them babies." So, I thought maybe Benita would work out.

On December 30, 2001, I was in my home in the hills sleeping in late with a lovely guy I'd met and hung out with in Mendocino. He came to visit. We were having a good time, having some grownup fun. It was the holiday season and I had a New Year's Eve show to get to in Vegas at the opening of the Green Valley Casino. The surrogate was scheduled to be induced a week later, January 7th. When I went downstairs at noon, I checked my answering machine for messages, the light blinking wildly.

*Hi Taylor, this your doctor. Just want to let you know Martha's water broke.*

What the hell? I look at the clock and it's 12:00 noon. The message had come in at 7:00 a.m. What the fuck? I listened to the next one.

*Hi, Taylor, this is the doctor again. It's about 7:30. Just want to let you know everything's moving along. Your surrogate is on her way to the hospital. I think you're going to be a mother today!*

At this point I was standing in my kitchen naked, with the phone in my hand, listening to these messages that continued to increase in frequency and intensity.

*Hi Taylor. I just want you know that Martha is here and comfortable in a room, her contractions are coming along nicely, it's 10 a.m.*

Shit! I was panicked. I called three of my girlfriends who were on baby duty, telling them what was happening and asking what the hell I should do. I didn't have a nanny locked down to start for another week. My assistant Dottie said, "Just hold on. We gotchu."

My friend Roseanna raced over as did Jenn to find me in shock, still standing in the kitchen holding the phone, still naked. Everything after that was a blur. My girlfriends talked to the guy still asleep upstairs and he was cool. Stan the man. Then Ro said, "Girlfriend, you need to put some clothes on and get to the hospital. You're about to have twins!"

One of them must have driven us to the hospital. We walked in like a crazed troop, with Stan right there with us. Christ, maybe he drove, who knows? We were quite the sight as we hurried in to find out what was going on.

In minutes I was thrown into scrubs and sent into the birthing room with my surrogate and the doctor to help her along. Levi was born first at 3:30 p.m. All yellow and shriveled and crinkly like a little old man. I cut the cord, we wrapped him and there was my son, in a hospital blanket and cap. Amazing! But Astaria wouldn't budge. For another 45 minutes we pushed, and Martha moaned and pushed until she screamed, "Get it out!" I was like WTF? A deer in the headlights. The doctor, all smiles and calm, says, "Ok, Martha, we have the forceps now so push." And with one good push and the forceps, Astaria was born exactly one hour later at 4:30 p.m. I looked through the glass of the birthing room to see Ro, Jenn, and Dottie smiling big and taking pictures.

Big questions needed big answers. Like Levi's name on his birth certificate. Levi Lotus Jeremiah Agustus Dayne. Yup, he was two boys alright. And Astaria Isis Dayne. (Father) N/A per Manchild's wishes.

The next question: Who is the nanny? But Dottie had that figured out. "Benita is ready!" That's all I needed to hear. I loved Benita. I'm like, "Well, tell her to pack a bag and get over to my house now!"

In 24 hours, the kids needed to poop and pee and weigh in at five pounds before they could be discharged from the hospital. I still had my New Year's show to do. Like the miracle babies they are, they cooperated, and 24 hours later we were in the car back to my house. The cribs and the twins' bedroom was so beautifully decorated by Roseanna over the last month, ready and waiting for those babies.

As we all jammed into their room, Benita was already in the rocking chair as she took both of those babies and held them and smiled big. "Ok, let's feed them!"

I had a bag packed and ready to head to the airport. I hadn't slept now in over 24 hours. Soon I was with the band in the limo heading to soundcheck. I was just staring at them. One of the guys said, "Taylor, you all right?"

Who knows? A mixture of shock, adrenaline, and excitement, and WTF. All I remember saying is, "Yeah, I think so. I'm a mother." The whole car erupted in laughter. "Hell yeah, you are!" I finally went to sleep 36 hours later.

Astaria and Levi were born in Los Angeles on Dec. 30, 2001 like all good little Capricorns to give me the tax break. Astaria had gray/blue eyes and dimples, and Levi had a mop of blonde hair. With their scrunchy-faced, innocently devastating power to heal, to make us laugh, to turn us to mush, they knocked out everyone in my street-smart family. I had wanted these children so desperately and fought so hard to bring them into this world, I was determined to give them all the love and security I never had as a child. My mom and dad, despite their less-than-perfect run as parents, are wonderful grandparents.

Every giggle, every fart, every next step was cause for celebration. Having babies in the house was like setting off a stink bomb full of joy. I've laughed at least ten times every day since they were born...and yelled, too.

And of course, there were the changes, the adjustments that having kids meant. One huge change was that Tikan was not happy. Like a jealous lover in my house, once they were crawling, he was nipping at 'em and growling, wanting to get them. I couldn't leave anything to chance. It was now my job to protect those two from harm. Like a momma wolf, I found my nine-year-old beautiful wild man a new home with other wolves on a ranch... and I missed him.

One chapter of my life closed, but another beautiful one had opened. And I was ready for it financially, mentally, and emotionally. I never really thought I'd do it alone, but here I was happy as hell. I took those two with me everywhere when I toured or worked on film locations, with me and Benita schlepping those damn car seats to bars, restaurants, and campers from NYC to Joshua Tree.

Over the years, I've been asked how I have sustained a career in the music industry over 20, 25, and now 30 years strong. You have to be flexible. In my professional life, moving between the worlds of film, TV, music, and stage was the answer for me. Investing in myself, recording and owning my own masters, building my touring business and buying real estate gave me multiple streams of income and more opportunities. I've learned that you can't be afraid to move when the cheese has moved. You have to be aware and open to new opportunities as a survivalist.

As a mom, I was more determined to let my battle scars be a victorious symbol of lessons learned.

# CHAPTER 7
## Hello, Goodbye

I FINISHED THE "Hi/Bye Letter"—the process my relationship guru taught me—all four parts, each necessary to go through and write about while waiting the required eight weeks before sending. Here it is.

*Dear* _____,

*It's been eight weeks since I last saw you or spoke to you. It's hard to believe. I feel it's important for moving on that I share my feelings with you, that I wasn't able to do during our relationship, through a letter.*

*Nowhere better to start than when we first met ... seventeen years ago...*

(This as PART 1, "What I loved about you")

*I met a bright, charming, handsome man with a huge smile and a strong laugh with a touch of naivete. You seemed happy, confident, and warm, and I felt good being around you. You were charismatic and generous and very open about your marital breakup and personal life. You had the bluest eyes and biggest grin. Later I learned a deeper sadness and conflict hid behind those eyes. You were smart, quick, and brilliant in business and negotiations. You had a degree, but you also had success in a career you helped define. You were very respected in your industry and by your late thirties had started thinking retirement. More than that, our similarities had a familiarity to me. You with your early successes as an athlete and running your own business. Yet with our styles very different, me from New York and you from California, I felt our values were in sync.*

You were well respected in your career at a young age, yet when I met you, things had changed in your personal life so dramatically. You had been knocked down off your perfect pedestal. Your impending divorce and life's curveballs had come down hard on you. By 2000 when we met, you had a more humble nature about you. You were empathetic and caring. I could relate your story to my own, having had success and fame at a young age and hit with a few curveballs I never saw coming.

As we spent more time together, I watched how you interacted with your clients and I admired your relationships with them. Having reinvented yourself early on when you had to walk away from your own dream, when an injury took you off the field permanently, you chose to go with your strengths behind the scenes. You excelled and that spoke volumes to me. I saw someone special.

We were friends first. I loved that. I had no desire to be with a man who was in a long breakup or just separating. I began to admire your integrity and ethics, and you held me accountable and reminded me that both parties can get hurt.

Your business clients prospered. I came from a more skeptical experience with management. Our similarities were that we both were gifted at a very young age and went for our dreams and made them a reality—me on stage and you an athlete.

Your protectiveness, your guidance, your nurturing, your brilliance showed action and care to those who worked for you. Most of your clients were friends. Opposites attract. You were strong in areas I felt weak. I loved that feeling, watching you shine and share that with me. I allowed myself a vulnerability I was not accustomed to with a partner because you were successful as well and I felt safe…like I could open up to you…you understood me. As we got closer, you offered nurturing and guidance. You seemed to be everything I wanted and more. My draw to you was one of the strongest pulls I've ever had for a man.

When we first met, we were both 37. I'd never been married. It wasn't a priority for me. I was married, as I realized, to my career, and you were in the middle of your divorce. What I did know for sure was that I wanted a child. When we met, I'd been single for months. Literally, I had dated my entire early adult life. Bad boys. Actors. Chefs. Models. Mechanics. Business men. MEN. I was not a naive girl.

I wasn't looking for a sugar daddy. Nor was I any gold digger. I had lived by my own rules, my own successes, my morals and ethics, and I didn't need a man to be in my life to just be a provider for me. I had done *a good job of providing for myself. I was a young woman who worked hard and gave it all to my fans and my music and my career. But now I needed more. Life had to have more meaning to me than more shows and tours and hit records. I had an ache that something inside me needed more fulfilling. And only going deeper into a relationship gets you there to that next level and could open this girl's heart.*

*By 37 I had gone through plenty and I was still standing!! But I also knew I was living a lonely existence and I was missing out on a soul connection. The "Why" question, the "What is this all for?" question was constantly weighing on me.*

*My biological clock was ticking overtime. Eventually I knew having a child was the answer for me. But being in a relationship with a man and marriage? I hadn't been lucky so far. Not for lack of trying. I had plenty of love and relationships and beautiful, great men in my life, but lasting? Not yet.*

*I had long believed that I couldn't be a mom unless I was in a marriage or a relationship or had enough relations to produce a child. Until when I was in the liposuction room, I believed that short of adopting a child on my own, I needed to be with a man in order to have a child. The liberation I felt when learning that I could fulfill my desire without having a relationship was huge. I needed to take different actions in my life. I needed to be a better woman. Before we met, I was making changes in my life. I was readying myself.*

*In the beginning of our friendship, you definitely were Mr. Charming who was looking to date, but I wasn't having it with you. I was dating and having a good time. When you asked me out, I said, "No way, you need to date like a motherfucker. You need to get out there and be with like 100 girls. You've been with the same woman since college."*

*You said you had been with plenty of girls already and separated for 1½ years. I said, "Not long enough to your 15 years of marriage." But you kept at it, saying to give you a chance, you felt more alive now than you ever had.*

(This is PART 2: "What else did I like about you?")

*Everything!!! How you looked, how you smelled, how you tasted, how you touched me. So this was IT! I knew to my bones. You were it for me 100%. I was myself—vulnerable, open, and sexual—with you. As we grew closer, there was often a blurred line as our lifestyles merged, but we* understood the complexity of the music, sports, and entertainment business we were in. I'd met my match on all levels.

I didn't see a self-destructive man. I saw that a few people around you were showing some signs. Did you not see this? It told me that maybe you didn't really pay close enough attention to their real lives, most centered around yours. Maybe it was that southern Cali suburbs naiveté. I thought you had a strong dash of street smarts.

I understood when we first met that you were going through many personal challenges in your life. I saw your desire to be open. You talked about your challenges and feelings of betrayal and pain from the separation you didn't want, the money you didn't want to lose, and the marriage you had thought you would still be in. How thankful and grateful you were to be on the other side of that pain.

You had your heart kicked in and you had buckets of humility. Now your ego was in check. Not such a bad thing. That's probably what made you more appealing to me and available. You needed people to help you through your pain. I found that endearing and loving. More importantly, as we spent more time together, I felt you adored me, desired me, wanted me, and that made me shine inside. The jock and the diva.

You were so into sharing your feelings with great amounts of warmth and attentiveness. We talked, we shared, we played, and then we made love. You would stare at me and then listen to me for hours, wanting to hear all my stories and learn more about who I was. I felt we shared hearts, sometimes even the same heart. I was so guarded when we first met. I had been dating my entire adult life. You were newer in the dating pool, but you kept at me and eventually you melted down my natural walls of skepticism by the desire you had for me and how secure you made me feel. I found a safe place; I found "The One."

As our friendship anchored, the days turned into weeks, and the weeks turned into months. Our families bonded, our friends bonded, our homes bonded, and our hearts bonded...so I thought. It felt as natural as the air to be with you. I was complete.

After two months of dating, I knew with certainty I wanted to be your wife. I knew I wanted to have your baby and I knew I wanted to walk hand in hand with you through life.

"I'm very in love with you, Taylor."

I felt the exact same way. And if this was your truth, I needed to share mine as well, I had been withholding a big part of my truth, so I went for it.

"I need to be honest with you. I need to show you a contract I signed with a surrogate agency. I need to tell you this because you're sharing your heart with me and I want to share my heart with you. I told you I wanted to be a mother and asked what you felt about that. I need to tell you and I need to know what you think, and do you want a child?"

As I handed you the papers to read that were in my hand now, I explained the five-month wait. I even said I had a donor for sperm. But why would I do that now? You're the man I was destined to be with. You are the father. You held my hand and said, "I've learned through my separation that I would never deny someone what they really want." You then held my hand and said, "Yes, please wait for me. Let me get through this divorce." I felt relieved, I felt blessed, and I was incredibly in love.

Of course, I would wait for you! All my dreams were coming true. I was on a waiting list. How long can a divorce take? The dye cast, your words your truth, written in stone for me. We were going to do it together. So, I waited, and I loved you. At 37, I felt a deep happiness and wholeness. I went to the edge of the cliff. Ready to jump.

I did something I'd never done before. I asked you to marry me. I wrote you a marriage proposal. I promised you my heart. I promised you my soul. I promised you my undying commitment and loyalty. I meant every single word I wrote. It was stored in the deepest cells of my body. I felt so completely certain and I needed you and I was not ashamed to say it. I needed to be with you always.

When I gave you the letter, we were traveling. We hadn't talked about the letter yet. Eventually I had to ask if you read it and what you thought. You said, "Yes, Taylor. It's very beautiful. It's just difficult because I'm not divorced yet." It never occurred to me before that moment and all that we had shared that maybe you might not feel the same way as I did. A seed of doubt flew into the universe that day.

Slowly and surely came the detangling and detaching. It started with you staying later at work, saying you couldn't make it to dinner. When I asked questions about our future, you wouldn't answer. I could feel your mind thinking, withholding. Your vagueness became more real. You weren't as communicative. You weren't as open. You became more guarded, and I became more nervous and anxious as you took the relationship backwards. Finally, you told me, "I don't think I'll ever marry again, Taylor. I'll never let myself get hurt like that again. I can't open my heart up like that."

You will never understand how painful it was to hear that from you.

*You, the only man who held every ounce of my hopes and dreams in the palm of his hand. It took me years to recover from that hurt. I gave you what you wanted, what you asked for, but you couldn't give it back to me in the ways that I could feel loved and cherished and wanted.*

*I didn't understand why you were pulling away from the world we had built around us. In my mind, in my heart, I believed in US to the core of my being. It was a belief that burned like a hope flame.*

*The dream was crumbling. You built a wall around your heart, brick by brick. Soon I was no longer the fun, passionate, strong, sensual beautiful woman full of life and laughter. It broke me. As I watched you retreat further into your old wounds and feelings for another woman I never even knew existed, IT became too real as you held on so tightly. I knew then "He's not in love with you, Taylor. He's not in love with you enough. He still has feelings for her. He's not certain. He's not sure. But you are."*

*So I reacted like I did when I was a young girl. I retreated. I left. I gave you exactly what it seemed you wanted most, your freedom. I retreated to my little house with my surrogate papers, back into the Hills. We broke up.*

(This is PART 3: "What I said I will never do again.")

*Then we reconnected 15 years later. I can't help but look back now 17 years since we first met, after being back in a relationship with you for the last year and a half. Again, I had to retreat back to my little house, still trying to make sense of you, of us, of what I will never be able to understand. The same questions...*

*What did you really want from me? Was I just a big mind fuck? A game? Was I just a curiosity? A challenge? See if you're lovable? If you can feel?*

*We had a love that was so powerful and so present. The two of us, one soul, our soul, the spiritual baby we made in the holiest of places. I thought it was the closest to God I had come with another human being. That's how it felt to me. We were together because it was holy—body to body, soul to soul. The union we created. Yet that wasn't enough for you or wasn't what you wanted, so I had to leave.*

*It took me three years to get over you. You would never be a father to our child, which ultimately became twins when my surrogate became pregnant four months later. It took me three years after you left my* house, at my LA baby shower, when you walked in and gave me a wad of bills up in my bedroom before you left and said, "That's probably the most money you've ever gotten, Taylor." I realized then you were gone, and you weren't coming back. I was a single mother to two babies. Alone on this journey.

Still I know that wasn't the hardest realization. The hardest for me was accepting how wrong I was about you. How my heart could be so wrong. That what I thought was my destiny was not. How my certainty wasn't certain. I thought you would love me no matter what, that you would fight for us. It taught me to doubt myself. I was wrong. Never again. I accepted the fact that our love wasn't real. I turned within and to my two beautiful babies just as I turn to them today, except that now, they're 15 years old.

As I left then, feeling unloved, I left you again, two months ago, after almost two years back together. You see, I'm not the same girl I was 17 years ago. You don't hold all the strings to the most important choices in my life now. I learned to do it without you. When we reconnected, you said, "I will never leave you. We're back together. These are my children. These are the children I never should have walked away from. These are the children I know as mine."

But here we are again, another woman between us, now another life you're still connected to. Add that to the last life you still hold on to, dragging these dead carcasses around with you like they're alive. No one will ever be more to you or will ever come first before you. I will never have all of you. I was just a mistress living in an apartment with you, not your wife, not living our life. But another version of your lives. Commitments never fulfilled, time always the enemy with wear and tear. A used car now fresh off the lot.

Never again will I push my feelings down and not express them. Never will I allow a man to neglect me and not check up on my well-being. Never will I allow myself to pretend for fear of rejection, the fear of being punished because it's not convenient. Never again will I allow a man to keep me as a lover and a mistress and not his wife. That is not what I wish. Never will I stay with a man who doesn't keep his commitments to me.

I need emotional security. I accept this about me. I need reassurances and mostly I needed you to take the actions you committed to me with.

I need it like water.

(This is PART 4: "Now thank him.")

*Thank you for bringing me this painful lesson so I can go back into therapy and learn how to never do this again.*
      *Taylor*

Of course, I wanted to sign it, "Love, Taylor." I wanted to say, "I love you, Taylor." I wanted to say a million things, but I just hit send. This was an eight-week internal battle night after night. Days of writing. What started as 22 pages was whittled down to 10, and then 8. Through the process, I was guided by my relationship mentor, Dr. Pat Allen. This was no small endeavor.

This letter took me weeks to write as I went through Valentine's Day and my birthday alone. Having no contact. In her eight-week program, Dr. Allen guides you through the process. She advised me to go back and revisit the hurt, go back into my heart and decide who I truly am and what I truly want. So, I did that; I did the internal work that was required because this was no small matter. When I walked out the door that day with my two teenage kids and a suitcase, I knew that was it. I knew if I left, I was leaving the "man of my dreams."

The first time around with him, my whole world was tied up in his hands. Going back 15 years later with two teenagers, my mind kept saying, "You're here, Taylor. You're still standing." After two years, when it came right down to it, I was not getting what I really wanted and what I really needed, which was the same exact commitment he denied me the first time. Now, armed with this knowledge and the support of my life coach and therapist, I came through it.

I was really proud of that. Not because I could walk away from the man of my dreams, but because I understood that this was a reward/punishment scenario. The ever-dangling carrot that he had no intention for me to eat. I would never be a good enough girl to get the gold ring.

Leaving was the most honoring thing I did for myself. I tried to make it work; believe me, I tried. I was there and I realize in the big picture, of course, this wasn't one-sided. I could be irrational and annoying, especially over those last six months. The pressure was building inside me, the anxieties of staying some-

**TAYLOR DAYNE**
132

where where promises weren't being kept.

I realized I couldn't be second. I couldn't do that to myself and at this point certainly couldn't show that example to my children. Because I know what my kids see is what they will become, because that's what their beliefs will be. I deserve more than crumbs, and I needed my children to see that. Writing that letter and doing the internal work that was required allowed me to break the chains of the relationship. And I realized that applied to almost all my relationships—including the one with my first love, which was my father, the man that I admired and looked up to while he was cruel with one hand and loving and sensitive with the other.

Most importantly, I loved myself more. My psyche so adapted to making room for the wounded, and I needed to break that cycle. The emotional rollercoaster isn't a ride I can allow myself to take anymore.

Now I've given to myself the life I want. I feel good. I love what I've created. I love my friends. I love and appreciate my parents. And of course, I love my children. I see in them a reflection of myself and of course their incredible, unique selves. And every day is hardly perfect, yet I get to do it better than the day before. I get to look them in the eye at dinner, with a full heart. Amen.

I've also learned that being an open book is not a bad thing. He would say that I was too honest, "Honest to a fault" his exact words. I think about that often, the blessing and the curse of speaking your mind, being blunt, not having a filter. I do understand in certain circumstances being truthful and honest is considered distasteful and uncomfortable. When I'm around people where the truth is difficult, it can be uncomfortable. And I can agree that some places and situations are not appropriate for one's own opinion to lead. Kindness is key, and you must know your audience and temper accordingly. But I've learned that in my intimate relationships, I do myself no favors nor my partner any when I hold back, with the exception of hurting someone deliberately with your words (which is not the best way to get your message across).

When I share my heart honestly, not in anger but with vulnerability when sharing is not an effort to control the outcome, as the chips fall where they may fall, how can that be a fault? If you are in a relationship that brings you to your knees, that's an opportunity for real honesty and truth. There are reasons I wasn't on my knees this time around.

This time I was standing, with two people I'm responsible for standing next to me. I feel obliged and protective. I didn't want them to see me fall to my knees and break down. I didn't want them to see me make decisions and choices based on fear of losing a man.

I also wanted them to know love.

*Taylor,*

*Thanks for your letter. I read it a few times and though I don't agree with a lot of what you said, I can respect this is your perspective and that if this is how you need to move forward and get closure then I wish you all the best, all the luck and happiness and success in this lifetime. You and the kids will always have a special place with me.*

*All my best.*

*Love, _____*

CHAPTER 8

# Born to Sing

HAVING A VOICE is one thing but being a voice for others ... well, that's something very powerful. All through my career, 1988 – 2018, I look at my audience. When you really look, you will find an extraordinary rainbow of people. I'm the little girl from New York with the big voice who stands up. That is powerful.

In 2016, I was asked to do a Ted Talk. At the time, I was exploring writing a memoir and went to work on finding "the voice within me" to do that. My night-owl hours and some late-night Google research led me to a teacher with a modern take on the written voice, Linda Sivertsen. Half blogger, half podcaster, half *New York Times* bestselling ghostwriter, she got shit done. Her voice spoke to me ... literally!

I wrote her a short note, and she fucking wrote back and said, "Let's talk," and just like that we did. Half book guru, half book mentor, Linda and her incredible writers' retreat in Carmel got me locked away with seven other magical women. Sometimes men come, of course, but not this time. It was all woman, all pussy power, all in different stages of writing stories. The golden Linda guiding, nurturing, teaching her publishing tools, contacts, "unicorn ideas." We would give birth, and she was our doula. And she meant business. The retreat was the exact medicine I needed to take the dive into the written word and walk out doing a Ted Talk?! WTF!

Yup, that was pretty much it. Cause within three weeks it was decided I would be a speaker at the 2016 TedWomen conference, a three-day event about the power of women and girls to be creators and change-makers.

I had six months to prepare a twelve-minute talk. What an experience. What a challenge. I had a massive responsibility to live up to, to share the stage with such brilliant women, all in service. I knew in order for it to be effective, I had to share a more vulnerable part of myself and my experiences that would be largely unknown: the message I wanted to share with other women. The weeks and months preparing for "My Talk" inspired me to write this book.

Enjoy it with images and songs:
https://tinyurl.com/TaylorDayneTedTalk

Following are my slide notes!

# Taylor Dayne
## TEDWomen
### 2016 Presentation

I love men...
I do...
I. Love. Men.
I might not like them very much sometimes...
I mean it has only taken me the last 50 years to learn how...
But I do... I love them.

And as I stand here before you today,
sharing with you some of my story...
This I do know...
Karma has been my greatest teacher,
and time my greatest lesson.

And that's the hardest part for me,
because I got no patience.

I mean, I'm a Jewish girl from Long Island...
I really got no patience.

So as I stand here before you today,
I can honestly say it's about (freaking) time!!!

Many of you know me as Taylor Dayne...
The singer...
The girl with the big hair, big lips,
and that big, ballsy voice...
Mmmmmmm...
My voice.

My greatest gift.
My greatest salvation.
My greatest tool.
My voice saved my life...
My voice gave me a life...
It gave me a purpose.
It showed me a way out of the chaos of my home.
It gave me a reason to push through my pain,
and push through my fears. Oh, and there were many...

My voice is my greatest tool
in what I like to call, my "Tool Chest of Life..."
*What's yours?*

You see, I believe the power of our greatness
lies in the very seed of our being...
in our DNA.

I believe we are born with "IT."
Every one of us.
Born with our own unique seed,
our own unique gifts.

Think back, if you can,
to a moment in time
you can remember ever being noticed...
recognized...
even admired for something you did.
Something you could do really well...

Something you created or achieved that was very special.
You shared it with others...
That's the gift.

Those of us who spent time with our gifts...
We planted our seeds...
We watered them...
We nurtured them...
Put them in the best light.
And over time, the seeds sprouted,
rooted, grew branches and blossomed...
These roots are the foundation of our life's purpose.
The blossoms bear the fruits of our dreams.

So, was I born with a voice?
Was I born with a gift? Or was it just "my time?"
Both.

A radio was the first gift that I can remember ever getting from
my father. Other kids got basketballs, baseballs, dolls. I got a
transistor radio. It had one music station: WABC New York. Oh,
yeah! The music they played on that station moved me so much
I sang along—people liked it when I sang along.

They said, "You're good."
And that felt good...
So, I got better.
So much better in fact that by the time I was 5 years old in
kindergarten they put me in the 6th-grade choir and
gave me a solo.

I sang every day after that.
Ask my parents.
The music became the loving arms I so needed,
the voices were my best friends.
The songs, a safe place for me to go.

I planted my seed...
And over time my voice blossomed.

TAYLOR DAYNE

As my life's purpose rooted,
I was recognized, and success came.

As I honed my skills,
I sharpened my tool.
A voice is a very powerful tool...
But so is a gift for numbers,
a gift for languages,
a gift for sharing ideas.

Do you know that every single I've ever released has the word
"love" or "heart" in the title? Yeah, it's true.
        "Tell it to My Heart"
        "Prove your Love"
        "I'll Always Love You"
        "With Every Beat of my Heart"
        "Love Will Lead You Back"
        "Send Me a Lover"
        "Can't Get Enough of Your Love Baby"

I mean, here I am singing to the world
about breakups and makeups,
love and loss...
and I've never even been *married*.
I mean, I've never even been *engaged*.
What's wrong with this picture?

FEAR.
*(Taylor sings "What is Love" by Haddaway)*

My father.
My brothers.
My lovers...
Give me Russell Crowe in *Gladiator*:
Strong and powerful.
Fighting for his family, his honor.

*(Taylor sings "Whatta Man" by Salt N Pepa with En Vogue)*
Or Mel Gibson in *Braveheart*:
Hounded.

Heroic.
Battling nations to avenge the death of his murdered bride...

Or Brad Pitt in *Legends of the Fall*:
Beautiful.
Tortured.
And you can see why...

*(Taylor sings "Close to You" by the Carpenters)*

And there it is....
Right there in Burt Bacharach's song...
My "why."

Why I so longed to be close to men.
My first love...

My father was a tortured man. And not in a beautiful Brad Pitt way but in an ugly, explosive and violent way. Unable to control his anger and rage, my father tore through our home daily yelling and screaming and hitting. His inner struggles to provide and protect for his family tortured him.

My parents grew up very aware of struggle. They were first-generation children of Holocaust-surviving parents. Survival and struggle they knew well, but our home wasn't often filled with joy and laughter, but more often tears and fears. My dad would rage, we would hide, and my mother was his perfect victim.

*(Taylor sings "I Never Loved a Man (The Way I Love You) by Aretha Franklin)*

Where was my knight in shining armor?
Where was my hero?
Who was my gladiator?
My father? He was too busy battling his own inner demons.
Yet sometimes late at night, after his rage ran its course, my father would come home and quietly come into my room. He'd kneel beside my bed and he'd weep...

He'd gently put his hand on my head and pet my hair whispering in the dark, "I'm so sorry honey, I'm so sorry, little girl."

*(Taylor sings "Do You Really Want to Hurt Me?" by Culture Club)*

"You're so special to me. You're my special girl. You know that?" Did I know that?  All I knew was...

*(Taylor sings "Love Hurts" by Nazareth)*

And yes, I did know deep down inside,
I did know I was special.

Cause I had a gift.
I had a seed...

And at 6 years old, I knew.
I would plant my seed and I would survive.

If my parents couldn't protect me, my voice would.

*(Taylor sings "BORN TO SING")*

# CHAPTER 9
## *Beautiful*

THIRTY YEARS LATER and I still feel like the little girl who has a lot to prove. It's just in my nature. But now with years of experience in the game, I have a sense of peace as I try more often than not to take the smarter-not-harder approach. I powered through my twenties and thirties like an ultra-marathoner. It says volumes about my strong work ethic; but also, I needed to be a part of the rat race, and eventually getting caught up without a game plan is a never-ending, exhausting ride. And something always burns out.

For me, when I turned forty my life became a whole other level of challenging. I had officially reached "The Power Decade." I was a new and very single mom of three-month-olds and batteries were not included. I felt the wear and tear. I needed help. I had Benita with me, thank God, but soon we needed weekend help and travel help. So, I added Blanca and Erica to the Dayne village. I needed the village, I needed the sisterhood, fuck it, I needed two nannies!

This I have learned from my children (Do not tell them that. Ever.). They taught me how to slow down and just be present in the best possible way, and they taught me how to never feel alone. Deep twin stuff. I'm not gonna sit here and say, "Oh, it's been easy raising two children on my own." That, friends, would be the biggest bullshit any parent could ever say to another. Single motherhood/parenthood is a trip, and in combination with being in the music business, it's crazy squared. Crazy cubed, with twins.

But what I will share from my deepest core is that being a mom has been one of the most gratifying, rewarding, and fulfilling experiences of my life. I can't even remember what life was like before Levi and Star. They are what inspired me to stay healthy, stay happy, and stay fit. And, hell yeah, looking beautiful and feeling sexy is all part of that well-being.

I was dating and loving and mothering; believe me I needed all the energy I could get. But without my sanity, health, and happiness, my house wouldn't run. Being a powerful female artist to me meant feeling powerful inside and out; feeling sexy inside and out, and mentally capable to navigate the ups and downs of life. It meant learning and leaning into a new awareness as I needed my body to sustain me and my children's livelihood.

The new demands on my body, mind, and soul took me out of my comfort zone. Being the only financial provider and legally responsible party for two other little human beings who had my made-up last name was often very scary. So, I took back control over the things I knew I could, like staying in shape and making my well-being paramount. This momma got oxygen, first as the life force of my family. I made it my mission to achieve optimum health and wellness.

Reinventing myself creatively was also a big part of that mission, and that meant releasing new music to tell the world about my latest journey into motherhood. It also meant Momma needed to tour and extensively promote the record. In 2008 I released *Satisfied*. The critics called the record a tour de force "sounding exactly that: satisfied, rounded, and whole." When the single "Beautiful" went to #1 on *Billboard* it gave me my 17th Top Ten record.

But as a woman in her early forties, I wanted love, I wanted to feel beautiful, and I wanted results, but my body wanted other things. I felt stuck. Really stuck physically for the first time. Weight was stuck to my body and wouldn't leave no matter how I tried.

As a girl I was very athletic in track and field and as a gymnast all through my late teens. I always had a good body; and yes, like a lot of teen girls I often went to extremes, unfortunately, like most of my girlfriends did in high school to maintain that perfection by purging, binging, and starving myself. Sometimes a yogurt a day. Sometimes 10 sandwiches back-to-back to be thrown up in an hour. Most of us girls were constantly low on self-esteem and confidence while riding through our hormonal changes and emotional waves. It was what we all did. I can't think of a day I didn't look in a mirror and judge what I saw. As young women we were constantly comparing ourselves to each other. We had an unspoken daily competition between our girlfriends, the scale, and the mirror.

In my twenties and thirties, I ran around the globe touring, making videos and movies, and taking pictures. I had wardrobe stylists, makeup and hair stylists. I had trainers and choreographers, and I even had a personal chef in Lisa Galotta who was cooking for me at my home, making sure the food I ate was part of the diet and fitness regimen I was currently on.

In my early forties as a working mom, I felt heavy. I felt thick. I saw thickness in my arms, my legs, my face that I hadn't carried around before. Diets would work for a minute—the fat flush, the cleanse, the cabbage diet. I still worked out. I have always worked out, but I was still thick. What changed? I was reading. I was researching. I was talking to other girlfriends around my age who were working in the business. What was I doing wrong and why?

In the past, if I dieted and worked out, I got the results I wanted within a week. I was firm. I had a good butt. I had muscle tone. Now it was not so simple. I had kids now, but I didn't carry them, so no excuse there for the added gain of weight. Why did my body feel like I felt? I was hearing a lot about hormone replacement therapy and bioidenticals and longevity clinics, HGH. I was curious, and I needed answers.

As I began putting pieces of my physical puzzle together, I realized…OMG! I might not have carried my babies, but I spent a lot of time taking hormone and fertility drugs while undergoing the fertility procedures for harvesting my eggs, which I did two separate times. I started seeing a correlation. The surging of my hormones from the drugs I took to match my cycle with the surrogate getting pregnant. Getting my eggs removed and harvested.

I did IVF at 39 years of age. While I was doing *Aida* on Broadway and eating controlled portions while on the Zone Diet. I was in five costume changes a night, in custom gowns made for me, performing eight shows a week for nine months while my surrogate got pregnant. My body didn't know what it needed to do to reset after a year of that, and I turned forty! Prozactly!

To me, my body was holding on for dear life. With so much uncertainly around me, my body was in fight or flight mode, storing up all the nuts it could to stay safe. All those hormones that were given to me stored up in different places throughout my body and never left. Now I had love handles. I had big boobs (thank you, Dr. Frank) and now I had back fat! I had no baby daddy, but I definitely had a butt roll.

One day the then-boyfriend says to me in the bathroom, "Hon, what's that lump on the back of your neck?"

"Huh? What lump? I don't see anything back there."

Well, he could, and it wasn't pretty. I went to a doctor, but not the right kind, at least not that time. I was told it was nothing. "It just looks like fat." Fast-forward a couple of years and a few doctors later when I landed in the right office to learn that the large lump growing on the back of my neck was really from an overproduction of Cortisol in my body, better known as a buffalo hump. Yup, the great white buffalo hump when your blood sugars are irregular and get spiked. Turns out it was from taking steroids given for chest infections, like walking pneumonia or bronchitis that any ENT will recommend so they can get an artist back out there and on the road. The long-term effects are staggering and detrimental to your health because they hang around in the body for a long time.

What I'm trying to say, folks, is that I spent a lot of money and a lot of time looking for answers from many different traditional and alternative doctors. And not until I found one particular doctor and source did I see any real significant changes in my body. She began to really target the physical, mental, and emotional issues I had been facing. She took the body as a whole, and after seven years of working with her, I can promise you this is the real truth...

YOUR:

- ✌ Blood don't lie
- ✌ Urine don't lie
- ✌ Spit don't lie
- ✌ Poop don't lie
- ✌ Guts don't lie (digestion/bacteria)

Analyzing your charts is key. Also, test your vitamin and mineral deficiencies in the spectrum test. It's crucial. Some minerals will prevent you from losing weight, so will bacteria and inflammation and mucus in your gut if not addressed.

Every body is different. Every body is unique. If you want a quick introduction, read the book *Eat for Your Blood Type*. That alone is a revelation. Most people don't even know their blood type. Find out. It changed my life. I was allergic to things I craved and that made me fat. Period.

All my friends know how important it is for me to share my enthusiasm for health, wellness, and beauty, and all the ways to achieve an ageless and timeless and youthful body, mind and spirit. Our energy is key. The energy we share with each other daily is key. Mastering and maintaining that energy is what keeps us vibrant and filled with life. How you disperse it and how you rebuild your energy (chi) is how you will maintain a great reservoir of continued source.

SO NOW I'M IN MY "fuck-you fifties." It ain't nature behind the perky boobs and great skin anymore. It's knowledge and sheer tenacity. All these years, carefully tending my scarred body, trying to make up for everything I felt I had lost as a little girl. These days I focus on maintaining this womanly body as the temple that protects my childlike spirit, and I have fun doing it.

My children drive me crazy and keep me sane at the same time. As Levi prepared for his bar-mitzvah, I found myself digging deeper into Jewish scripture and tradition, searching for answers that resonated for me and a teaching and wisdom that stuck. With my torch readings, my life coach, my incredible circle of powerful female friends, a full touring schedule, and lack of restraint when dropping F-bombs, I know I'm not exactly the average mom. But I invest all my faith and every ounce of my very limited patience into this family on a daily basis and my kids know it.

That's where I find myself today, thirty years into this musical journey of life. Hungry. Ambitious. Hard-working. The last fifteen years working for me and my family and my fans. Enjoying the ride more now than ever. I love performing. I love mentoring. I love seeing how my music elevates the energy in a room, and I am honored to be a part of that process. Being an artist, I love being part of the community of artists as we continue to activate, celebrate, and motivate through music.

The recent loss of Aretha Franklin was hard for me. Her voice elevated the listener, a scripture all its own, a gospel she spoke through her voice that all women could relate to. As many other important music figures have passed over the last few years, it puts things into perspective for me as I stare at 30 years in the business. I question my own legacy and take responsibility as I continue to push my voice where it needs to serve, and now with my speaking voice as well. Thanks to Tig Notaro and TEDWomen. A successful, single, working mother, a sister, a boss lady, a mentor, a BFF, a celebrated female artist and "an underrated voice in the music industry." Yeah, I've read that often enough, too.

In 2018, *Billboard* magazine announced their list of the Top 60 Female Artists of All-Time. Number one Madonna, number two Mariah, number three Janet, number four Whitney, and the list continues. Where am I on this list? Smack in the middle at number 35. Taylor Dayne. I'm on that impressive, inclusive list after Celine Dion (#25) and before Tina Turner (#37). Seeing the amazing women on this list gives me another piece of the puzzle of my career by putting things more into perspective. By honoring the work I've done, the hearts I've touched, and the impact I've made on music and in people's lives, that's so incredibly gratifying. It fills me with joy.

I've learned to embrace music streaming on Spotify and having a presence on social media with Instagram, Facebook, and Twitter to continue my journey, to see where the cheese moves and adapt when I need to. I must be willing to adapt to the changes in the industry to stay in the game. I'm proud to still be here. In private, quiet, still moments, I think how comfortable I am with who I am and where I am. I feel full and I like me.

In 2018 I released my 30th Anniversary Deluxe Album, created a viral video, and wrote this book. I also performed around the country almost nonstop. It's all about sharing myself and hoping my story connects with you in some way. That's my job as an entertainer, whether I'm on top of the charts or not. When I'm on stage, the audience gets a glimpse inside my heart and soul, and with these other projects, hopefully you will learn even more. The journey continues beyond the hit records.

Maybe at this point in my life, I've learned to let go and not be so analytical and practical. If somebody asks me to sing, I generally do. I've learned that what I do brings people happiness. It makes people feel good and hopefully encourages them to do good. You never know who you're sitting next to and what they are dealing with. When I share myself with others, it makes me happy, too. Recently while sitting in a small club in Boston, grooving with the band late one night, people started coming in from the street, the staff came out of the kitchen. "I know that voice." The ripple effect in full bloom and all of us under the same roof lifting it together.

My voice: the one constant in all my journeys, what saved my life and continues to sustain me and bring joy. It's something I have never taken for granted, even when I was a child, and I will continue to nurture and care for this incredible gift and tool that I was blessed with. To do that, I must sleep. I need down time to recharge, to shut down and block out all noise and retreat into silence so that I can regenerate. It's really that simple. It mostly prevents me from talking too much, too.

With "Tell It to my Heart" there's a timeless classic to embrace and truly appreciate as Taylor Dayne, and I will forever be tied to that unmistakable melody. People always ask me when I knew that I had "made it." I'm never sure how to answer, because I don't think that anyone ever realizes at a certain moment that they are at the pinnacle of their success. I have learned to find a way to take it all in. Oftentimes it happens for me when the people I care about remind me. So I stop, and I breathe to take it all in, and my heart fills with gratitude and light.

I was in the studio the other day with a young, emerging producer who's doing amazing work. His manager came by to say hi to me and posted a photo of us on Instagram after, to do a shout out that his client was in the studio with "the legendary Taylor Dayne who is celebrating 30 years in the game." That's when it becomes real, when others remind me.

TIME HAS ALSO ALLOWED ME to put other things into perspective. What I went through with Clive and the label, when things were good, they were great. He took me under his wing and guided me. His joy was to be around music and its greatness and to share that knowledge, often to a fault. I've made peace with that over the years, and I understand it better now than I could then. Maybe it was his approach, but when I felt controlled like I did with him, I reacted. It was instinctual. The tiger in me came out. I wish we could have worked together in a way that allowed us both to feel respected and appreciated. I was just not used to receiving without expecting something bad to happen, the old hug and then slap. I'm sure I manifested that more then I care to admit. And I don't acknowledge that just because had I realized it sooner, I might have had a few more hits; rather, because it would have helped me grow as a person. Sooner. But everyone goes at their own pace. As Lisa G. would say, "Life is a go-at-your-own-pace party." I had to ride it out and learn how to manage the inherent distrust I developed at a young age.

RACHEL IS SOMEONE who reminds me of myself at her age, although I was on stage and behind a mic by then. At 22 years old, she is poised to break big behind the talent in the business. She's energetic and enthusiastic, which is an important part of the equation. I had my notepad and pen with me because I'm always studying and learning myself. So, I asked her, "How can I help you? What do you need?" She talked, and I listened to her talk about her contacts, her influencers, her enthusiasm. I saw the fire in her. I also see a lot of girls at 22 get distracted.

I told her, "Every day you have to write and take notes. Do it daily. Every night I then read through my list and check off what has been achieved and what has not and set goals for the week. I write and rewrite my notes on a clean sheet every day. I see what my intentions are for the day, for the week, and review the deadlines I've set. If you write down your goals, it keeps them visible as a reminder. You can use your iPhone or whatever works, but you have to be disciplined and focused. Do. It. Daily."

In October of 2018, I was invited to an event organized by the Creative Community for Peace. It was held to recognize SB Projects founder Scooter Braun, Geffen Records President Neil Jacobson, and Warner Music Group Global VP of A&R Aton Ben-Horin as "Ambassadors of Peace." All under the age of 40!

Rachel was there and is working hard to break big into the business side of the entertainment industry. And in some ways,

I've found myself in a sort of mentorship role with her. And I appreciate that. She is already worried about not getting her foot in the door. "Neil Jacobson is only 35 years old and he's president of Geffen Records."

I said, "You know what he and everyone in this room has done?"

"What?"

"They took risks. Every one of them is an entrepreneur."

"But my parents are concerned about me having benefits and healthcare." Oh boy.

"Rachel, I understand that, but that's what you get in a corporate job. You can have that, but that's not this life."

She smiled weakly. "I know." She had even taken the initiative to volunteer at the event in hopes of being put in some opportune situations. She's ambitious AF.

I told her, "In this business, you must think like an entrepreneur. You must bet on yourself. You must take risks now, not focus on health insurance. You're 22, for God's sake." She had told me a few days earlier that she wanted to quit and get a "real" job. "That's certainly up to you," I said. "It has to be your decision. You gotta want it bad because you will hear 'no' a lot more than you will hear 'yes' in this business. I'm willing to help you and do whatever I can, but you must do your part. To be blunt, you have to eat, shit, and sleep this business twenty-four/seven. It has to be your mission statement. I'm willing to take the risk with you but remember that it *is* a risk. There are no guarantees. Trust me on that."

She nodded. "That's all I do anyway. That's what I want to do, but it's embarrassing to sit here with a volunteer badge on like this. All I want to do is network in this room. I have to just trust that I'm going to be successful."

"There you go," I told her. "That's the entrepreneurial spirit. Give yourself a window, if it's six months, eight months, and set some goals that you need to achieve in that timeframe."

She said, "What are my parents going to do, not support me?"

"You can't go back and forth. You can't go into it knowing you have a safety net. People might tell you to fuck off, but if it's the right move and you hustle, the money will come."

"You're an incredible inspiration and mentor, Taylor."

Me: "I'm your mentor?"

Her: "Yes, you've helped me so much."

Wow. I was sharing with her some of the hard lessons I learned, and I realized that this is an important part of what I do. There's no denying that I've seen a lot and learned a lot. The time is right to pass that on to others, so they may be spared some of the painful decisions I had to go through. Rachel watched intently as people came up to me at the party to talk or just introduce themselves. I could see that she was paying attention.

"When they come up to you, you can tell that they love you!"

Did I mention she's a sweetheart? I said, "Maybe. Just know it's a business. You are valued based on your popularity and ability to make money. Listen to these young gentlemen who are literally the top in the industry at 30 and 35. Learning from others who have taught them, sometimes fathers, sometimes mentors in business, but all of these guys were young and saw something that others didn't. They took risks that paid off."

All I've ever done is take risks and believe in myself above everything else. To me it was my only option. Drive and enthusiasm can get beaten out of you if you let it. Those old patterns and old beliefs never completely go away. As you learn and grow, they eventually fade to a background noise if you know what they sound like. Enthusiasm and drive aren't things that can be taught. That has to be part of your makeup. It has to be part of you. That entrepreneurial spirit, in part with a philanthropic soul. The importance of giving back and sharing knowledge helps others.

Back to my daily accomplishments, I have other lists as well. Keeping them visually in front of you is a tool I use for a variety of important areas in my life, ranging from music and work goals (like getting this book finished) to investments and personal growth. You need to visualize it. You need to see it first, then you need to own it. Be it.

One list is to remind myself that I am:
- ♥ Cherished
- ♥ Desired
- ♥ Nurtured
- ♥ Protected
- ♥ Cared for
- ♥ Safe
- ♥ Present
- ♥ Capable

And so it is. I'm never going to allow myself to be in a position where I don't have control over my own destiny. That goes for work and relationships. I've worked too hard to let that happen. And ain't nobody going to believe in you until you believe in you. Then start to fan the fire with some small wins. You'll see you're soon on your way. If your energy is not strong enough, you have to work on that. That's your vitality.

I have a close relationship with a man who teaches entrepreneurialism at MIT, and he has shared some of his insights with me. He was mentored, and he in turn mentors many. I've learned that mentorship is a natural extension of what I've been doing on stage for years. I never really thought of it like that before, but every time I get behind the microphone, I am out there sharing my truth, what I believe in. I am able to share that with people in a way that inspires and excites them, and more importantly makes them happy. That realization and personal growth has saved my life in this industry and given me the fire to continue to perform and share.

I don't know where that came from, whether it was after studying Kabbalah or going to therapy or getting back to nature. It's probably a combination of the modalities I've incorporated into my life such as Pranayama breath work, meditation, and motherhood. I suppose that's what 30 years of hard work gives you, a renewed perspective. I'm sitting on something a little bit richer than ever before, and I enjoy the feeling of accomplishment, of actually saying, "Wow, you have done what you set out to do and much more." That's huge. I couldn't call it security, but that realization has brought me more peace.

Even at this stage of my career, I keep putting in the work. I don't let my focus shift or get derailed. I also keep working on myself. When I need some clarity, I visit my life coach. I trust her ear and knowledge, and I know she will help guide me in the direction that is right for me. Sometimes, all we need is a different perspective to provide another view that we haven't considered. I always leave those visits with a bigger tool chest of knowledge and a more loving and compassionate understanding of just how far I've come.

Baby, you're beautiful.

CHAPTER 10

# Love Will Lead You Back

THROUGHOUT MY LIFE, the most important thing I've worked through and learned to do is love and trust myself. That wasn't always easy. As people come in and out of your life, some for a season and some more permanently, lessons are learned, big and small, the hard way or the easier way. You choose.

I feel lucky to have some special folks that are still around. I feel truly blessed revisiting friendships that are forever and whenever we see each other, we can pick up where we left off. And I honor the ones who didn't make it and the connections that didn't have legs.

I've been through enough personal and professional relationships to know the difference. I'm in my third lifetime, really, when I look at myself as a novel or play. Not all relationships turn out the way you would like them to, but each taught me something about myself, and I wouldn't be the person I am today without going through those experiences.

Today, my parents are a big part of my life. They are deep into their 80s and I'm often moved to tears with gratitude knowing my children got to have them as part of their entire childhood. My parents were an active part of the family for Levi and Astaria when they were young. The kids now travel to Miami to see their grandparents or my parents come to Los Angeles and visit us, or we meet in the middle.

"The cheese" moved years ago so I moved along, too. Amen that I was able to see that, and I treasure the time I get to spend with them.

My brothers Hugh and Rob still reside in New York; one in the city and the other with his family in Long Island. And yup, we still talk to each other like we're 15- and 16-year-olds, stupid brother and sister stuff, deep, funny, animated, family talk. LOL. You gotta love family.

The Russian boyfriend and I continue our tradition of wishing each other a happy birthday and have done so for the last 35 years.

Manchild still lives in London and now is a married man with a wife and three children. We all stay in touch, and he and the kids have a nice relationship.

The Chef moved from New York after we broke up and opened his first restaurant in Miami, then Vegas, and continued very successfully. We remained friends up until recently when he sadly passed away from an unusual blood disease. Our couple's therapist is still "our" friend and confidante.

Terri Rojers and I never really saw each other very much after she left the business. We did speak a few times over the years and I even saw her kids, but our friendship and bond had ended.

Joel Lennane, my dear friend and road manager, passed away while working with Maroon 5, doing what he loved and what he did best...caring for his artists.

Several years ago, I wrote Clive a letter telling him that while I didn't feel good about his methods, looking back I could understand what he was trying to do. I apologized for my part in our disagreements, and I hoped that he is happy. I never heard back from him, but I know he received it, because later I was invited to his Grammy party.

♭

FEAR WAS SOMETHING I learned early, like a mother tongue that came naturally. It was the language spoken in my home. My father, my mother, my brothers, and eventually my lovers—as much as I longed to be close to them, the people in my life left a scorched path of blessings and wreckage.

But this I know as surely as I know the words to all my own love songs: Love is the final frontier. Amazing things happen when you allow love to outgrow fear. I've witnessed this throughout my life and the lives of others, so I have to believe that if I go forward without fear, the love I'm ready to receive will be a magnet for the love I'm ready to give.

It's not about fairy tales or being swept off my feet because it's not about them. Really, it never was.

# *Epilogue*

I'M IN AN UBERX leaving LAX. First call I make is to the kids. "You up? I'm on my way home."

Next call is to my friend Celeste, "What's up?"

She says, "Let's do a hike. Hurry up!"

Me, "Should I get the kids and we all meet at Bagels and then do Coldwater?"

Celeste, "Yeah. Move it!" And promptly hangs up. I laugh when I hear silence.

I'm coming home to throw on workout gear, grab the kids and climb a mountain. Why? Because it's Sunday. Family day. Yup, pretty much the exact same torture my parents put me through growing up. Sunday is "Family Day!" God, how I love it *now*. I love every moan, every "Mom, please," "I have cramps," "I don't want to hike! GHHHAAAAD!" I love every complaint, as these soon-to-be 17-year-olds get their asses out of bed to greet their mother.

Celeste is already on her way to harass and motivate them with "going for bagels," a normal Sunday in the Dayne household. I'm usually just getting off a plane after some weekend warrior travel tour dates, rallying the kids up by noon to greet me, then we hike and eat bagels, or we eat bagels and then hike while we laugh and moan (the kids) with each step as Celeste and I walk and talk our business, relationships, who's a shit, and what we're doing for dinner later. Who's cooking, or do we just say *fuck it* and do the usual and head to Noodle Monster for the best hot and steamy bowls of Pho in the valley?

Next, we text the crew to see what's up—Cynthia, Lori, who's around and if they wanna bomb over. And that's pretty much the day. My village. My happiness. Work. Home. Blessed.

AS WE BEGIN to contently eat our bowls of soup and dumplings, shoving six people into a four-top now that Lori rolls in, Levi makes an announcement that he has his driving test tomorrow. We all stop mid-mouth and look at him. "What? When? Where? Don't you have school? That's Monday!"

Levi, "Yeah, I do. I'll go after. Umm, yeah, I signed up last week. Umm, yeah, I can do it." This is boy talk and code for a conversation being held with a 16-year-old young man. Nuts.

I'm like, "Little dude, when were you planning on telling me? Do you have a set time and place?"

Levi, "Umm, yeah, I have it. I know where." Silence.

I say, "Hmmm, cool. You gonna tell us where cause last I checked, you need a car to take a test."

"Ummm, yeah, I think it's somewhere in Van Nuys."

All of us, "VAN NUYS? Why the hell there?"

He smiles that cute little blonde football-boy smile and says, "Oh, cause, ahhh, yeah, it's like the only DMV I could set up a test with last minute before Thanksgiving."

I'm like, "No shit." Levi wants his driver's license. I want a million dollars. We both want it bad. "You know, Levi, I have appointments set up tomorrow, too. Like you go to school, that's your job and I go to meetings! Tomorrow I have a big meeting before Thanksgiving break in Beverly Hills at Maverick Records. So, unfortunately, no, I can't give you my car to go to a DMV halfway across the world to take your driver's test. I'm sorry. I wish you would have talked to me about this. I can't be there for you and take you. And why would you book a test at 1:30 p.m. on a Monday when you are in school?"

"Mom, I need my license. It's for your convenience. When else can I take it? Just sign me off last period."

Unbelievable, this kid. Oh, Levi, he's a smooth one. Very charming, making all us women laugh. "Ha ha ha, very funny. Well," I say, "I can't take you."

Celeste immediately jumps up and says, "So what if he misses a class. I'll take him."

I'm like, "What? Celeste, you're such a sucker for his BS." Ha ha, yup, she's laughing, Lori's laughing, Cynthia's laughing. He's got four intelligent adult women right where he wants 'em. Eating out of his hand. It's really unbelievable.

Celeste then says, "Take an Uber from school, Levi, and I'll leave the office and meet you for your test. I'll meet you at the DMV at 1:30 and you can use my car." I look at her. "Just go to your meeting," she says. "Don't worry. We'll be fine. I got him."

I'm so SMH, watching the charm and BS ricocheting off the walls with him, and she just loves it. And Levi? He's smiling away, eating his shrimp wanton soup. This kid.

I said, "Celeste, he's gonna show up to take his driving test in Van Nuys in a Range Rover? Jesus Christler! They're gonna fail him before he parks. I know if some 16-year-old kid showed up for his test in a RR for me, I'd fail him just because *he needs to take a shit box car.*"

She says, "Well, tough. Too bad because this is all we got."

It's just unbelievable. Alrighty then, you've got it covered. What could go wrong? Well, he's going to the DMV. It's Murphy's Law. When going to the DMV, what can go right? For three weeks the kid was carrying around every single paper he conceivably needed to take the test. I know that much. I did my job making sure he didn't lose anything. I just wasn't counting on Celeste showing up for him without anything like her license and registration.

THE FIRST TEXT COMES IN from Levi at 1:30 p.m., his test time. "Mom we got a problem."

Dear God. "What?"

"Celeste forgot her license."

I'm like, "What? No!" It's too insane to take in.

"Yeah, she needs to have proof she is a legal guardian and owns the car."

The next text is 10 minutes later. "Oh yeah they said her license plates are registered in Louisiana. So, I can't take the test in her car because it's not registered here."

Then, "Umm yeah, like, she brought no proof of her registration with her. And it's also expired soooo can you come here?"

"WHAT??!! I'm gonna kill her."

Leaving my meeting happy and calm, now I'm racing on the 405 freeway to get across the hill to Northridge. Waze says I'm 30 minutes away, God willing.

I call her. "You guys are unbelievable—"

Celeste cuts me off, "It's so crazy here! You can't image how crazy they are at the DMV!"

I'm like, "Of course they're crazy at the DMV! They want blood! How did you forget your license?"

"I don't know, but I did."

Fine. "I'm on my fucking way, but will they let him take the test later?"

Celeste, "Yeah, he's been flirting with the girl at the desk so she's gonna give him a window of time for you to get here before they close at 4:30. So move your ass! We're waiting." She hangs up. Unbelievable.

I finally get there and realize, shit, now he's taking his test in a newer Range Rover. This is not good.

"Get out," she says. "Give him your car to go get on the line to take the test. They've been waiting for him."

Ahh yeah, no shit, I just drove here, crazy person!

"Mom, where are the lights?"

What? "One would think you'd know, Levi. Did you read the manual?" JESUS H. CHRISTLER! "Here are the high beams, the parking lights, the wipers…" I'm like losing my shit. This kid, how did he get the learner's permit?

Celeste says, "Everybody just calm down. You get out of the car. You're getting him too tense." I'm getting him tense? I'm gonna kill him! "Just get out of your car and sit in my car. I'll do it with him. Here's the keys. You're too aggravated."

"I'm aggravated? Fine," as I march off to her car illegally parked in a motorcycle spot.

It's 3:45 p.m. I sit in her car. I take some breaths. I calm down and look around. I see a guy and his fruit cart on the corner. This is medicine that I know works. It's hot out, its mid-November, and there's a guy selling fruit cut up and cubed right in front. Fresh-cut watermelon with fresh-squeezed lime drenching the fruit and hot chili powder sprinkled on top. Oh, happy day!

I buy two single-quart containers and walk back to the car happily munching away the hot day while waiting and waiting and waiting. My mind drifts off as I wait and think and float above...

*Thinking about motherhood...I did become a mom and I did do it all in a very unconventional way, that's true. I did hire a surrogate. I did all the fertility. My kids are my eggs and an ex-ex-ex-lover's sperm. I chose not to carry for different reasons: 1, I was not in a solid relationship at all, and 2, I had severe bladder and kidney mechanics issues as a child that left me scarred. I didn't think I could support a full-term pregnancy, but by 38 I most certainly was ready to be a mom.*

*Thinking about my kids...I have a million things to tell you and share with you whenever you're ready, Beautiful. I'm always available for you. I mean it. Truly. I love you. Meanwhile here's a little reading when you get a bit of time so maybe you can understand my journey more and why I made some choices the way I did. ~ Mom*

As I regain focus and my mind clears and centers, I see Levi walking slowly towards the car with a big-ass smile and a signed paper in his hand. I can't help it. I smile, too.

Oh, happy day...

♡

# Photos

Highlights from Taylor's life and throughout her career.

♡

Photo of Taylor with her father.

Family photos from the author's collection.

Family photo.

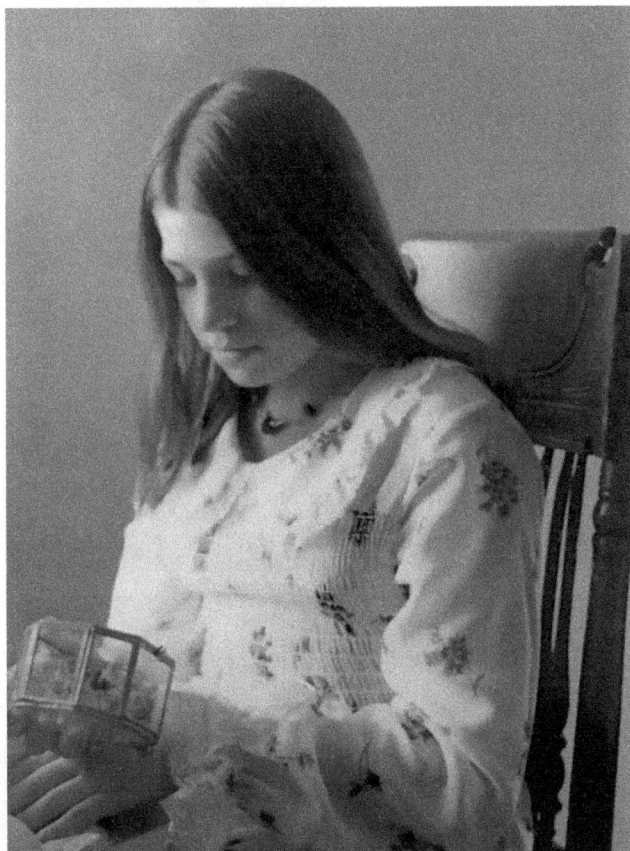

A young Leslie Joy Wunderman, from the author's collection.

Family photos from the author's collection.

Taylor onstage at the Odessa, Brighton Beach Brooklyn, NY.

Taylor with Tommy Burns backstage prior to hitting the stage
in Barcelona on Michael Jackson *BAD* tour, 1988.

Taylor performing at The Bitter End, NYC.

Promotional handout from the author's collection.

In Germany with Bela.

Hanging out with friends.

Photo shoot in studio at
"Top of the Pops" on
Nov. 5, 1987 in England.

©Sherry Rayn Barnett

Onstage, "Top of the Pops" November 5, 1987, in England.

Robert Plant and Taylor backstage at Tynes Tees, The Roxy, February 11, 1988, in England.

Taylor with Clive Davis and team at Arista for Double Platinum "Tell It To My Heart."

November 1989 in Dortmund, Germany.

1988.

November 1989 in Dortmund.

"Can't Fight Fate" tour, 1990.

Taylor signing "Soul Dancing" for fans at
a record store in 1993.

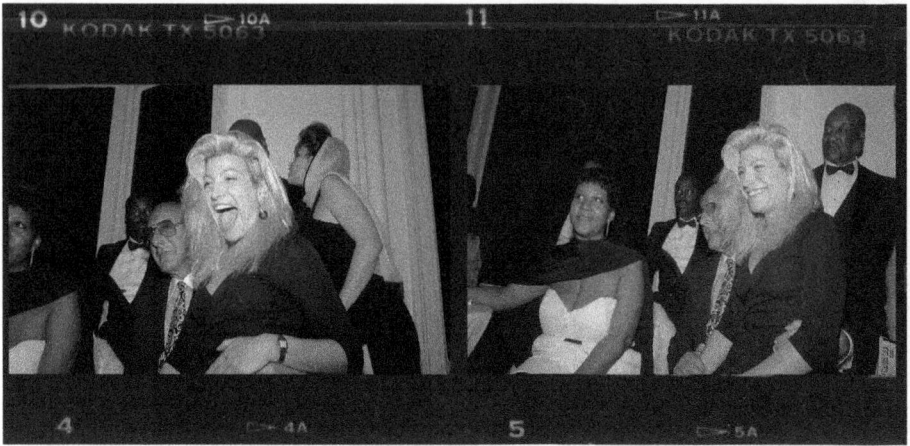

Aretha Franklin, Clive Davis, and Taylor at a party in July 1989, New York City.
First frame shows Whitney Houston in background.

Photo taken of Taylor at the Berlin Wall.

Taylor and her manager Frank DiLeo in 1990.

Photoshoot 1990s.

Taylor performing at Club USA, New York City, 1993.

Taylor celebrating her 30th birthday with Kelly Cutrone,
her father, and Lisa G.

Film still from "Stag" circa 1997, with Taylor and Kevin Dillon.

©United Archives GmbH/Alamy

Tower Records with "Naked Without You" in the window.

Photograph by Bert Stern outtake from the photo session for
"Naked Without You."

English singer-songwriter Lisa Stansfield, Clive Davis and Taylor
at Arista's 15th Anniversary Concert Benefit at Radio City Music Hall
on March 16, 1990 in New York City.

©Waring Abbott/Getty Images

Teddy Pendergrass and Taylor
photographed on Jan. 22, 1991 in Los Angeles, CA.

© Globe Photos/ZUMApress.com

Working on the film "Love Affair" – Taylor, Annette Bening, and Chloe Webb, in 1994.

Olivia Newton-John, Thomas Dolby, and Taylor get together at
United Nations, where they performed for an international fund-raising effort
called "Spirit of the Forest" to save tropical rain forests – June 1, 1989.

Kevin Aucoin / Sean Cheesman
makeup                choreographer.

Makeup artist Kevin Aucoin, Taylor, and choreographer Sean Cheesman.

Taylor's Polaroids from the "Can't Fight Fate" photo shoot
with photographer Wayne Maser.

Photograph ©Matthew Rolston

Taylor's Polaroid from the photo shoot with photographer Matthew Rolston.

©Ron Galella, Ltd./WireImage/Getty Images

32nd Annual Grammy Awards on February 21, 1990
at Shrine Auditorium in Los Angeles, California.

The Mansion.

Taylor with her horse on Long Island.

Taylor under the full moon
camping in Ojai.

©Dave Lewis/REX/Shutterstock

John Enos and Taylor attend screening of the
film "Instinct" in Los Angeles, June 1, 1999

©Matt Baron/BEI/REX

Taylor and Quentin Tarantino
at the world premiere of "Snatch"
held at the Directors Guild Theater
in Hollywood. Los Angeles, CA
January 18, 2001

Fun with Roy Uwe Horn and friend!

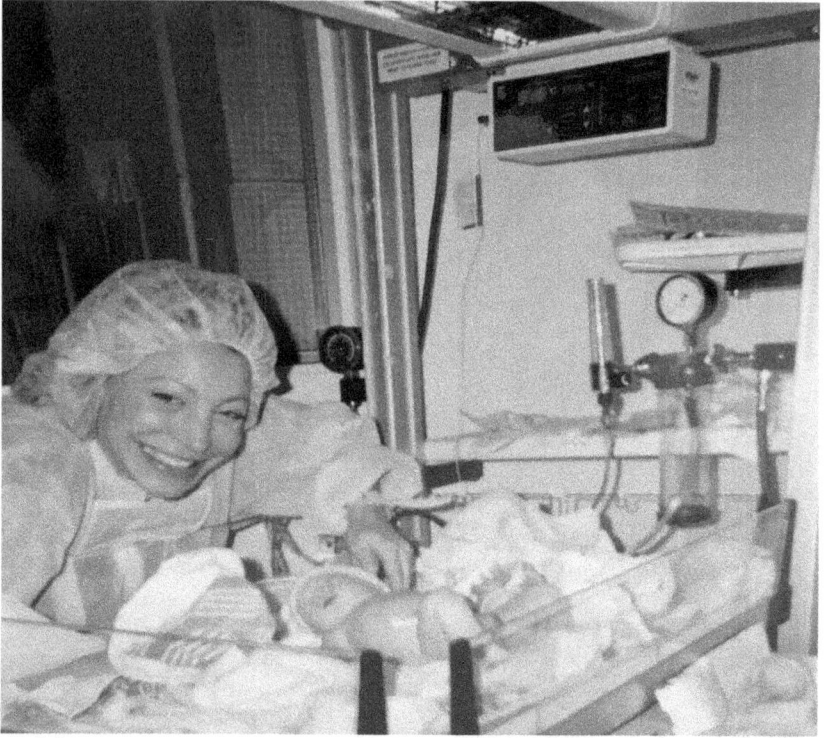

Birth of Taylor's twins!

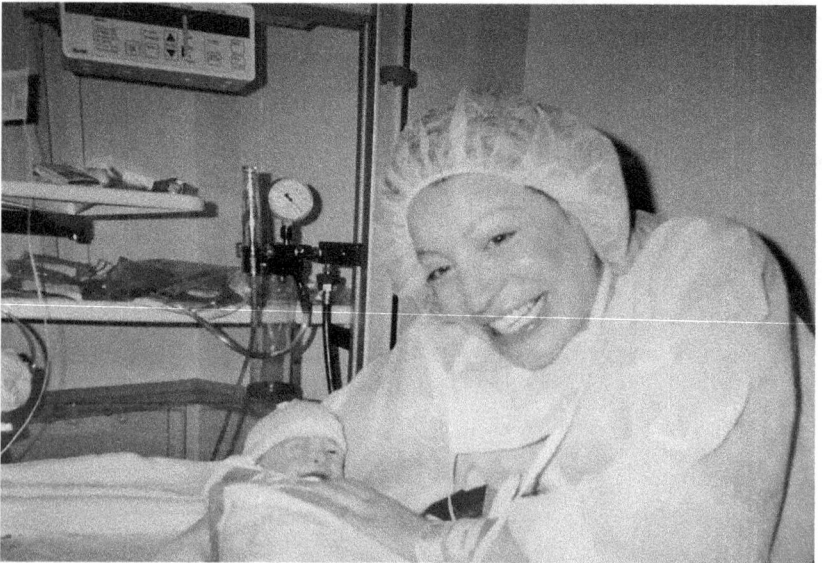

Taylor and the twins.

Taylor with son Levi and daughter Astaria at
Nana's Garden in Beverly Hills.

Astaria and Levi.

Family photos from
the author's collection.

Taylor at Joshua Tree.

Fishing in Wyoming.

ABOVE: Taylor howling with her wolf, Tikan, as a puppy (nine years before twins were born).
LEFT: Taylor playing with Tikan in the backyard.

Hanging with Roos in Australia.

Taylor with her NY girls at Kentucky Derby Churchill Downs.

Performing at LA Pride.

©CHRISTOPHER AMERUOSO

Designer Kenneth Cole, Taylor, actor Mario Cantone, and Dr. Mathilde Krim attend the 9th Annual amfAR Honoring With Pride Celebration at the Hudson on June 9, 2008 in New York City.

Photo by Joe Kohen/WireImage/Getty Images

Taylor with friends in December 2009.

Dinner at Cheryl Tieg's home with Marianne Williamson, Amy Smart, Francis Fisher, and BFF Jimmy Demers.

Taylor with Stanley Clark and Chick Corea.

Comedian Tig Notaro tells a story during "This American Life" performance about repeatedly running into Taylor. Taylor's singing walk-on during the show was a great comedic moment!

Taylor with Brett Michaels on the tour bus.

Musical artist Kate Pierson, honoree musical artist Adam Lambert, Taylor, and founder of WAFF, Nile Rodgers attend 2013 We Are Family Foundation Gala at Hammerstein Ballroom on January 31, 2013 in New York City.

The Temptations, Paula Abdul and Taylor in 2013.

Travis Tritt, Taylor, and Kid Rock at Barnstable Brown
Kentucky Derby Eve Gala 2013.

Taylor as Grizzabella selfie while performing in CATS 2013.

Taylor, Diane Warren, Clive Davis and Leona Lewis attend the premiere of
Apple Music's "Clive Davis: The Soundtrack Of Our Lives" at Pacific Design Center
on September 26, 2017 in West Hollywood, CA.

Singer and honoree Smokey Robinson and Taylor attend The Thalians Gala
benefiting Operation Mend at U.C.L.A. and honoring Robinson
at the House of Blues on Saturday, April 26, 2014 in West Hollywood, CA.

Taylor and her band perform at the Paradise Artists Party during Day 4 of the
IEBA 2014 Conference on September 30, 2014 in Nashville, TN.

TAYLOR ♥ PHOTOS

"The Colors of Christmas" with Taylor, Peebo Bryson, Jennifer Holiday, and Ruben Studart.

Quest Love and Taylor attend Sixth Annual Hamptons Paddle and Party for Pink Benefitting the Breast Cancer Research Foundation at Fairview on Mecox Bay, August 5, 2017 in Bridgehampton, NY.

Photo by Patrick McMullan/Patrick McMullan via Getty Images

Taylor performs at The Pompano Beach Amphitheater
on March 17, 2017 in Pompano Beach, Florida.

From the author's collection.

A selfie, hanging off the boat, traveling along the
Amazon River (Happy Girl).

ABOVE and RIGHT: From the author's collection.

Taylor with PEPA.

Super Freestyle Explosion concert at the Watsco Center in Coral Gables, Florida, featuring Taylor, March 10, 2018.

JLN Photography/WENN.com/Alamy

Taylor with Lisa Lisa before performance.

Taylor with Wendy Williams after performing for Wendy's birthday on her show, July 18, 2018.

Photo by Fadil Berisha.

# Acknowledgements

*I want to thank these people for their continued support,*
*guidance and enthusiasm throughout*
*birthing this book.*

Thank you...
To my agent Todd Shuster,
To my manager and friend Konrad Leh,
To the never-ending enthusiasm of my publisher Nancy Cleary,
To my attorney and friend Larry Verbit,
To my brilliant Life Coach Simone Bienne,
To the brilliance and essence of Joni Rogers,
To the wisdom and execution of Dave Smitherman,
To the amazing photo work by Laura Hanifin,
To Linda Sivertsen and her Carmel Retreat,
To my brilliant team of ladies... Norma, Rachel, Joanne, Andi,
  Kara, and Whitney.

To my incredible and remarkable children Levi and Astaria Dayne.
To my parents for forever supporting my dreams.
To my brothers Hugh and Robert.

To my Tribe of Friends & Family...I love You and I need You...
  Celeste, Onetta, Shelly, Michelle J, Jamyse, Michelle B, Lisa M,
  Kelly C, Cynthia, Lori, Mel, Nicky, Lisa M, Lisa G, Joe, RJ, Jason W,
  Jimmy D, Roseanne, Gracie, Lisa A, Debra, Lorenza, Brenny,
  Aura, Patty, Nancy, Diane M, and Chris O.

And to my incredible Fans for your love and commitment
  and extraordinary voice in this world—thank you for
  giving me a platform to perform for you these last 30 years.
  I. Am. Forever. Grateful.

And to all the men I've loved...

www.ingramcontent.com/pod-product-compliance
Lightning Source LLC
Chambersburg PA
CBHW032044080426
42733CB00006B/191